NEGOTIATION BLUEPRINTING FOR BUYERS

fact based negotiation with case study examples

by

Rosemary Coates and Brian Dietmeyer

Edited by Diane Vo

Rosemary Coates

For our families, friends and colleagues
with whom we are always negotiating

Contents

Foreword by Brian Dietmeyer

It may sound cliché but the very nature of buying and selling has changed dramatically. Some of this change is due to the global economic shifts, the availability of data and the changing role of both buyer and seller. While some economies continue to struggle, others are expanding at a rapid rate. Additionally, the availability of supplier data, software that supports turning that data into insight has shifted the buy/sell process and created a dynamic where both sides have more information earlier in the negotiating process. Sellers are being trained to place more emphasis on selling solutions that solve customer problems and create true measurable business value. Buyers are being asked to source products and services that are in alignment with and support of specific company strategies, key initiatives to forward that strategy and improvement of operational process.

All of these shifts point to the need for a change in the way buyers approach negotiating deals with suppliers. With the advent of these changes, it's time to think of a new paradigm for supplier negotiation. Part of that paradigm shift is reframing negotiation as decision making. As a professional buyer it is incumbent upon you to make decisions on supplier selection and negotiate final deals that are in alignment with corporate strategy.

- You make decisions on which supplier provides the most overall value for our company

- You make decisions on how suppliers get compensated in exchange for that value

The key enabler for enhanced decision making is data. In this sense, data is understanding the needs and business drivers for multiple stakeholders on both the buy and sell side. At Think! Inc. we think of negotiation as a very complex decision. There are multiple stakeholders in both organizations that are evaluating multiple aspects of their alternative to reaching agreement as well as evaluating the terms for reaching agreement. In a typical negotiation there may be 40–50 moving parts.

1

One other paradigm shift is something we call "reverse selling." In our work over the last 16 years we've seen that the most difficult negotiations are those with strategic or single source suppliers. These are situations where it appears the supplier has more power due to the difficulty of high switching costs or simply no viable alternatives. What we will talk about is how to increase our leverage in these situations by becoming a more strategic and valued customer.

The approach we will prescribe has to be "consumable" by those who use it. Many negotiation-planning processes are too complex and just not realistic for us to execute given our daily demands. In this book, we have narrowed down the negotiating data to that which really matters. We have embedded three major concepts into what we refer to as a Value Blueprint. This Blueprint and the data that populates it are the underlying structure of every business deal. It expands and contracts in relation to the time you have and the complexity of the negotiation. We have attempted to build in as many case studies as possible to move this from a book that talks theory to one of practical application that helps make better business decisions.

Finally, this book is written by two people with 50 plus years of experience on both the buy and sell sides of deals. The benefit to you as a reader is an understanding of holistic thinking and analysis based on multiple internal customer needs on our side and multiple stakeholders on the sales side.

Introduction by Rosemary Coates

I was first introduced to Think! Inc. in 2008. A colleague set up an initial phone call with Brian Dietmeyer, the CEO of Think! Inc., to explore the possibilities of joining the team. At the time, Think! Inc. was primarily focused on training salespeople. But I had always worked and consulted on the buying and operations side of business, so I was interested in what the company could do for buyers. In preparation for the call with Brian, I ordered *Strategic Negotiation*[1] from Amazon.com and spent a weekend reading and thinking about the Think! Inc. methodology.

As I read through the chapters, I became completely intrigued. I had never seen anything like this before. The methodology was simple and elegant and it made perfect sense. I knew buyers were going to love it. I couldn't wait to talk with Brian about building a procurement practice. So it began.

Since that time, we have trained many buyers in the Think! Inc. methodology, with outstanding results. Our clients report negotiating deals with much greater value for their companies and vastly improved supplier relations and cost savings. Most importantly, buyers who have been successfully doing their jobs well for many years tell us that Think! Inc. opened their eyes to creativity and results they never imagined were possible and, as an added bonus, made their jobs a whole lot more fun.

The negotiating method and tools we teach are simple and more of a toolset instead of the check-off lists taught by other companies and consultants. This approach is so much more appropriate for today's buying environment where buyers are more sophisticated, better educated and more thoughtful in terms of the needs of their business.

Since the 1980s, industrial buying has gone from getting three quotes and executing a three-part carbon paper Purchase Order typed on an IBM Selectric typewriter, to a sophisticated electronic environment where information is available at the buyer's computer command. With

---

[1] Brian J. Dietmeyer with Rob Kaplan, *Strategic Negotiation: A Breakthrough Process for Blueprinting Business Negotiation* (Chicago: Kaplan Publishing, 2004).

3

the introduction of ERP systems buyers can now assemble historical buy information, supplier history and performance, develop RFPs, RFQs and enable reverse auctions. Electronically, buyers can exchange offers with suppliers and transmit Purchase Orders via EDI. Procurement is now taught at the undergraduate and the graduate levels as part of Supply Chain Management programs at universities around the world. Students emerging from graduate programs are more strategic thinkers and have a much broader understanding of businesses as ecosystems.

Sellers are also getting more sophisticated. By doing online research, they have a much better understanding of their competition and of their company. They can quote from your annual report and cite your CEO's direction for the near future. Through email they may be talking to many other people in the company, selling to the business and bypassing Purchasing like never before. They too, are better educated and sell value-based solutions. Gone are the days of taking buyers to lunch and expecting a purchase order in return.

And finally, deals have changed. Today, deals are rarely about just one price for one product. Buyers now find themselves buying products and services that include software, maintenance agreements, training, field service, supplier-managed inventory and a host of other things. Requirements are based on tight forecasts, Sales and Operations Planning (S&OP), and Lean principles. Buys are likely to be international, whether the buyer is purchasing from a local distributor or buying directly from overseas. International buying is complicated by currency, culture, communications and global time zones. All of this means more complexity in every buy as well as many new opportunities for far better negotiations.

Oh, how the buying world has changed!

Part 1: The Think! Inc. Methodology

Overview

Negotiation is often incorrectly diagnosed as a soft skill that is based on verbal tactics. There is also an incorrect assumption that negotiation is random. If you believe that these are the problems of negotiation, then you prescribe long lists of counter tactics and emotional staging. How do you remember, implement, or scale dozens of ideas and checklists?

If you believe that negotiation can be anticipated and controlled, then you prescribe a different approach—one based on analysis and strategy.

In *Harvard Business Review*, Danny Ertel wrote, "I have found that companies rarely think systematically about their negotiating activities as a whole. Rather, they take a situational view, seeing each negotiation as a separate event, with its own goals, its own tactics, and its own measures of success. That approach can produce good results in particular instances but it can turn out to be counterproductive when viewed from a higher, more strategic plane."[2]

In other words, organizations without an organizational negotiation strategy and process for executing that strategy one negotiation at a time, are letting their tactics and deals present a picture of who they are in the marketplace by accident rather than by design. Furthermore, we are not using negotiation to enable aspects of our organizational strategy.

That's why we encourage you to "redefine" how you think about negotiation as just one blueprint, and three concepts.

When you follow these concepts, you'll be better able to:

- Complete higher value buys
- Complete buys quicker by shortening the negotiating cycle
- Lower total cost of ownership
- Connect your company strategy to your tactics
- Improve internal customer relationships
- Increase power in single and strategic source situations

---

[2] Danny Ertel, "Turning Negotiation into a Corporate Capability," *Harvard Business Review* (May 1999).

Why Now?

With the implementation of ERP systems and Supplier Relationship Management (SRM) systems over the past 20 years, the demands on procurement have become greater. Now the cause and effect relationships of production planning, requisitioning, buying, receiving and payables are all part of one continuing process. Buyers are recognized as a very important link in the supply chain and your performance is monitored not only on cost savings but also on how well you manage suppliers and keep the right materials in stock. Through this evolutionary process, buyers have become more professional, more strategic and better educated.

Suppliers have become more sophisticated, too. Gone are the days when a salesman would pat you on the back and take you to lunch in exchange for a type-written Purchase Order. These days, salespeople offer solution sets and focus on providing value to your organization.

So it makes sense that the tools you need for effective negotiations are also changing. The Think! Inc. approach is based in analytics and follows a blueprinting process that will teach you to architect deals and maximize your savings and value.

Defining Negotiation Time

Most buyers would define negotiation as that time when you are sitting across the table working through the terms and conditions of a buy. If you are waiting until that time, it's too late. Let's say that this is a typical buying cycle: you understand the buying criteria, do some data collection, you implement your buying process, and then the negotiation takes place… or does it?

If we wait until that point in the buying cycle to begin negotiations it is too late because the supplier's behavior changes when they perceive that they are now negotiating, and so does ours. We start holding our cards close to the vest, view the situation as Us vs. Them, and try to drive down the price. When formal negotiations begin, the supplier stops sharing information and both sides start to focus on themselves.

Negotiation Is Highly Strategic

Negotiation is not tactical; it is highly strategic. The way we negotiate underscores what we believe about our company, our brand and our value. Think of the many transactions that you have been involved with over time—what you expect, what you give away and what you choose to protect. All of these transactions message your suppliers, competitors and shareholders about what you believe regarding your value. You can protect, or unravel, your brand equity by the way you negotiate.

You can also do better. Not only can you achieve more savings in your buys, you can add value that will win over the hearts and minds of your internal stakeholders. Through the process of blueprinting, you will learn to evaluate what is important to your internal stakeholders and business partners as well as to your suppliers. But to achieve this higher level of performance, you need to start early in the buying cycle.

Negotiation is a continuous process, not an event

A good buying process helps us to be sure we have qualified the right supplier, have uncovered key decision makers within that supplier, are creating a solution that is connected to our business strategy rather than just a product, and we are delivering the most value for our company.

Whoa, wait…key decision makers inside the supplier's organization? Many of the procurement organizations we work with at Think! Inc.

are used to dealing with the supplier's salesperson. But in fact, there are probably key stakeholders inside the supplier organization who are interested in more aspects of the deal than just getting a PO by the end of the quarter. We mentioned "reverse selling" at the outset of the book and we'll have more about that later when we talk about the Consequences of No Agreement (CNAs) and Trades.

A good negotiation process will help you continue to create value for our stakeholders and then protect, or get credit for, the value of the solution presented. It should also allow you to define the deal on your terms and get most of the savings; probably more than you are achieving today without a strategic approach and methodology.

Dr. Max Bazerman, co-founder of Think! Inc. and professor at Harvard Business School, likes to say that negotiation is about good decision making. Good decision making is about data and knowledge. Use data you gather from your buying process to get yourself better organized, thoughtful, analytical and proactive.

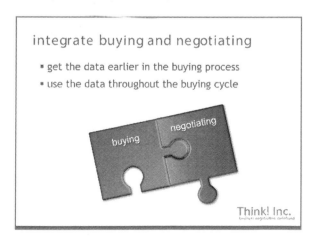

To be considered "world class," we need to view negotiation as a continuous analytical process, and embed it early in the buying cycle before anyone is even thinking about negotiating!

Every buy is different in terms of people, size, complexity and emotion. But the underlying structure of a buy will ALWAYS remain the same. This is part of Think! Inc.'s evidence after studying 20,000 negotiations and how people made negotiating decisions. If you can get your head around this underlying structure you will be able to clear away the clutter and simply analyze the key components of any buy.

Sourcing and Buying Internationally

Sourcing and buying internationally is also very important in today's international buying environment. You are probably sourcing internationally or buying from distributors that are sourcing internationally, and the blueprinting approach applies to all of these situations. The fundamentals are the same across cultures and negotiations.

While the setting and execution may vary in different cultures, fundamentally the three concepts remain the same. The process has validity no matter where your source is located. In our many years of sourcing and negotiating in 43 countries on both the buy and sell side we can confirm that the blueprinting approach will always result in better, faster negotiations.

Take China, for example. Negotiating with the Chinese looks different: more people, more rounds, more strategies and nothing is finalized until all the details are clear and the negotiation "picture" is set. Westerners often find negotiating with the Chinese to be frustrating and takes way longer than expected. But the fundamentals of the Consequences of No Agreement, trades and anchors are ever-present and will help you favorably close the deal faster.

Redefining Negotiation

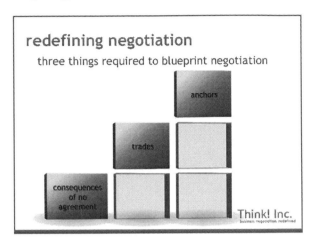

The Three Concepts

The negotiation blueprint starts with the Consequences of No Agreement or: what are all the consequences to either side if there is no buy? In negotiating, people will make a decision to take a deal provided it is better than their alternative. This is our first concept to understand. This is where real value comes into play for your company, making optimal decisions on suppliers that further your organization's objectives.

Next, we look to grow the financial pie (agreement zone) as large as possible by trading valuable things in and out of a deal. We do this first before we worry about dividing the value and determining who gets what. This step informs our decision on terms we can accept in exchange for value provided.

Lastly, we anchor the negotiation in a frame that allow us to claim as much of the value as possible.

> *Life is simple, it's just not easy.*
> Eric Fellman, The Power Behind Positive Thinking

Consequences of No Agreement

In any negotiation, the other side always sees your offer as a gain or loss based on its perception of the consequences of not reaching agreement with you.

Buy Side

What will happen if there is no deal with the supplier you are currently in negotiations with? How valuable is your alternative? These are the questions to ask your internal stakeholders and to determine for your supplier. This is the Consequences of No Agreement (CNA) for each side that defines the limits of the negotiation. That is, what are the costs and benefits of your alternative if you walk away from the deal? By defining the outside limits, you will know the Agreement Zone within which the deal can and should be made.

Many of you are aware of this concept known as BATNA (best alternative to negotiated agreement) from *Getting to Yes*.[3] Think of CNA analysis as BATNA on steroids and supercharged by extremely relevant data.

Determining CNAs is going to take some research, some conversations and some work. To identify the CNA for your side of the deal, you will need to ask your internal stakeholders what is important to them and what would happen if the deal does not get done. In fact, more specifically, you will ask internal stakeholders, given their current business strategy, key initiatives and desired operational process improvements:

---

[3]   Roger Fisher and William L. Ury, *Getting to Yes: Negotiating Agreement Without Giving In*, ed. Bruce Patton (New York: Penguin, 1991).

- What are the criteria to use when attempting to choose one supplier over another?
- How important are each of those criteria to cross-functional internal stakeholders?
- How do alternate suppliers (or methods) score in meeting those needs?
- On average, which supplier or method meets your strategic and operational goals better?

The following list of supplier performance metrics is from "The Supplier Selection and Management Report 9/01" from the National Association of Purchasing Managers (now the Institute of Supply Management):

- Financial stability
- People
- Supplier performance
- Supplier cost reduction ideas
- Supplier development projects
- Delivery
- Quality
- Product cost
- Order accuracy
- Customer support
- Business relations

These are the things buyers use for analyzing their Consequences of No Agreement (CNA). As you can see, not only is price not the primary concern, but it is number eight on the list!

We were executing this kind of brainstorming with a global airline looking to source inventory management software. We had five different internal customers in the room. As we began to brainstorm this list the commodity manager claimed that cost was the highest ranked criteria, and the vice president of Engineering proclaimed, "Cost is not the #1 issue, I don't care how big a discount you obtain. If it doesn't effectively automate my warehouses, we paid too much!"

Different internal stakeholders in your organization will provide different criteria and weighting based on the organization's needs at this moment. Think! Inc. can help you develop these criteria and make better decisions. Many times it is the very discussion with stakeholders about their business objectives, criteria and weighting that improves not only the negotiating plan but also our credibility with them.

Example

Stakeholder	Criteria	Weighting: High (H), Medium (M), Low (L)	Supplier 1 Score: 1–10	Supplier 2 Score: 1–10
Finance	ROI	H	6	7
	Cash Flow	L	10	3
	Liquidity	M	8	2
Operations	Delivery	M	3	5
	Service	H	7	8
	Support	L	4	2
Marketing	Brand image	H	1	4
	Joint marketing	L	1	3
	Promotions	M	10	7

The above type of analysis allows you to execute a weighted average score for each supplier and determine which one meets your needs best. This information Is used to inform your negotiation plan on what investments and risks you're willing to make to have access to their solution.

Identifying your own CNA in this way, will help you to define the limits for the deal and Agreement Zone. That is, if the deal doesn't get done, what is the impact to your organization? What is most to least important? How heavily are those things weighted relative to the needs of other stakeholders? How does each supplier stack up on average? Does the supplier meet multiple needs on average better than your alternative?

This provides the most value and can inform the second stage of negotiation, determining how much you are willing to compensate that supplier.

This information, or "Consequences of No Agreement," is the first step in blueprinting.

Consequences of No Agreement
Seller Side

Suppliers measure the value of our offer against their CNA. As buyers, we need to present value in a language the supplier understands. Most often, the supplier will do a deal if you can help them to: increase revenues/margin/share, improve processes or reduce risk and, of course, if the deal is better than their CNA.

The next step then is to define the CNA for your supplier as best as you can. Ask yourself, what will be the consequences for the supplier if the deal doesn't get done? Of course, there will be the financial impact of lost sales, but are there other components of the loss that you can identify and quantify? Or, in other words, what criteria should your supplier be using to decide to accept or reject your offer?

There are three good ways to determine your supplier's CNA:

1. Ask the supplier

2. Do your homework on the Internet

3. Gather information internally

During your meetings or conversations with the supplier, ask what the impact would be if the deal does not get done. Typically, the supplier will enlighten you enough for you to determine their CNA. Of course, losing the deal has a big impact to the salesperson, but how else will it affect the supplier? To gather this information, you will probably need to speak with other people in the supplier's organization; we call these reverse sales calls.

Visit or talk with the supplier and meet with Sales and other key stakeholders and ask about their priorities.

• What are their current high level business strategies?

- What kind of business metrics are they trying to move?
- What key initiatives are in place to drive strategy?
- What operational process improvements are they attempting?
- What are the characteristics of their best customers? (Most sellers have ideal customer criteria that go well beyond volume and price.)
- How do you match up to their ideal customer criteria?
- How does losing this deal impact all of the above? What is their alternative?

Use supplier site visits or phone calls to gather as much Information as possible about the supplier's top priorities and interests. The information you gather will help to determine the supplier CNA. In many cases you don't have to do these visits yourself but rather set up "suit-to-suit" meetings with VPs of Engineering, Logistics, Finance and Sales from both sides of the deal.

In addition, do some research on the Internet about the supplier and the industry. What challenges are they facing? Determine what issues are important to the industry. Review what is written about the supplier and what they have written about themselves. This research may provide some insights into their CNA.

For example, if the supplier's industry is going through regulatory changes, you could determine how your business might impact the changes they need to make. Perhaps a joint approach to new regulations would be valuable to both sides.

Example

Stakeholder	Criteria	Weighting: High (H), Medium (M), Low (L)	What is the Impact to them of losing this deal (+) or (−) or (=)
VP sales	Revenue Goal	H	−
	Roll out of new product	L	−

Example (continued)

Stakeholder	Criteria	Weighting: High (H), Medium (M), Low (L)	What is the Impact to them of losing this deal (+) or (−) or (=)
VP sales (continued)	Their image internally	M	−
	Can they replace you with a better customer	H	+
CFO	Cash flow	M	=
	Ability to invest	H	−
	Forecast	H	−
COO	Production capacity	H	=
	Usage of assets	L	−
	Inventory	M	+

When we do this analysis we get a sense of those areas of importance where the supplier will feel negative impact if you don't agree with them. It's not only revenue but their ability to meet strategies, such as rolling out a new product or service, impact on their capacity, etc. In those situations where we are not a strategic customer for them or where we are in single source situations, we want to execute an objective analysis to determine where losing the deal will have minimal impact. We also want to look at those areas where losing the deal might actually be a plus for them. For example, if they are running at full capacity and can replace you with a customer more in line with their schedules, it could be a plus. To become an ideal customer, this analysis shows where we need to work to make ourselves more strategically important and to gain more power. This is also very powerful information to share with your internal customers to build a more objective negotiating plan.

Use this background to spark discussions about the supplier's CNA and their priorities.

Defining CNAs allows you to determine what the impact would be if there is no deal and to define the place where both sides prefer agreement to impasse, based on both sides' alternatives. Any deal within the Agreement Zone is going to be acceptable for both sides. The key is to capture as much of the Agreement Zone as possible for your side.

One of the biggest problems we see is that buyers are making decisions based on one or two key criteria out of context. In fact, Benjamin Franklin wrote that the problem with making decisions is that all the pro and con reasons are not present in the mind at the same time. It is the Value Blueprint that allows for optimal decisions by having all pro and con reasons in mind at the same time.

CNAs for both sides must be quantified as much as possible. You need to know the financial and strategic impact if no deal is made. Whichever side has the least financial or strategic impact has the most power in the deal because they have the least to lose. But even if you do not have the most power financially or strategically, you create power by analyzing the situation and controlling the negotiation through the use of data. Dig for as much data as you can find: internal reports of deliveries, quality, invoices, etc., plus external data from your meetings with the supplier, Internet research and other sources. Use all of this information to create a profile of your supplier and their industry, and to build and test their CNA.

Remember, the best negotiations are based on analytical approaches, not emotional ones. Information and analysis in a negotiation creates power.

You must be careful not to measure value through your eyes only. There are two sides to every deal; It's important to consider value for the supplier's side, too. This will help you understand what makes a great deal for both sides.

Before Think! Inc. engages with any new customers to train their buyers, we execute a negotiation diagnostic to get a sense of the current and desired state. One of the areas we see as problematic is that most buyers have their best relationship with their front line sales rep. This is okay for day-to-day deals on commodities that are not strategic for your firm. However, in strategic or single source situations where you are attempting to increase your power by becoming a more strategic customer, a relationship strategy is of utmost importance.

As a buyer, your role is often to be a businessperson first. This means keeping your eye on the big picture of how your organization, and your supplier's organization, can work together. A good habit to get into is to think through all of your supplier's strategies, metrics, key initiatives and operational goals. It might be helpful to talk with a co-worker, internal stakeholder and your supervisor about your supplier, as they may be able to provide additional insight. The better you identify the supplier's CNA, the better it will help you determine which supplier provides the most value.

Executing CNA analysis should be done on every deal; for simpler negotiations this might take 15 minutes. For more complex negotiations, it may require you and five to six internal customers in a room for several hours. It is also helpful to think through your internal customers' and supplier's criteria in advance of asking them. This extra effort on the more strategic opportunities allows you to more proactively control the negotiating process and add value internally and externally.

Because negotiation blueprinting is a process, these steps get easier over time. Before you know it, you'll have a system in place to work through both sides' CNAs in draft format, rather quickly in advance.

Using the Blueprinting Process in a Large and Complex Negotiation

Let's try out this part of the process on a "live deal" involving thorough analysis around the two aspects of the negotiation blueprint.

It's April 1st and you're preparing to communicate to your preferred supplier that after all your months of trying to get to closure on buying some of their machines, it's finally down to a choice between them and your CNA (their competitor). You will ask them to put their "best foot forward" proposal in six weeks, by May 15th. You also hint that their competitor is aggressively pursuing it, is being quite creative on price and has a pretty good product fit. Before you issue this formal challenge, you complete step one: CNA analysis for you and your supplier.

Step One: The Consequence of No Agreement (CNAs)—Your Supplier

You complete an overview of the supplier's CNA and determine that if you don't reach agreement with them you will choose their competitor and they will lose the business. In this case, you estimate losing the business means that...

- The supplier loses about $750K in global revenue in the first year. If, however, you take into consideration potential long-term revenues for this supplier, total CNA costs could be as much as $2.5M.

- The supplier loses the costs associated with the four months they've spent selling to you—approximately $25K for staff time, product demonstrations, etc.

- Will have some soft costs in the form of "political heat" from their Vice President of Global Sales and the head of their product management group, both of whom have a personal interest in this sale as it impacts their bonuses, as well as the salesperson's bonus.

- Losing this sale will, in effect, fund a competitor by sending these revenues to them.

- The good news for your supplier is that the market is growing—albeit slowly compared to past years. The chances of replacing your business are fairly good and you get the sense that their list of other prospects for sales looks good at the moment.

- Also, while you believe they have no other customers that are this large and ready to close, you think, based on your discovery with them, that there are at least two or three smaller ones that they feel positive about. All of them together could replace this sale, but it's always more profitable for them to close and service one customer than several.

Step Two: Consequence of No Agreement (CNAs)—You and Your Internal Customer's

As always, attempting to analyze your own CNA is easier. In this case, you know your CNA is to go to their major competitor, and, probably, pay less. What's tricky, though, is the total analysis—that is, determining the positive and negative effects—of you choosing their competitor. The first thing you do is pull together a team from your side. You invite several internal customers who have a stake in this deal, a person from Engineering who just came to you from the supplier's organization and some additional product experts. You give them an overview of the situation and ask them to help you brainstorm all the decision criteria you should be considering when comparing the lead supplier to your own CNA.

After brainstorming, you ask the group whether, from their perspective, each element is positive or negative compared to choosing your alternative. The team breaks down the analysis in terms of design of the solution, delivery and installation, ongoing maintenance, output and long-term upkeep. The results of their analysis suggest the questions that must be addressed are:

Design Elements:
- Is there an "off-the-shelf" solution that fits our needs?
- How much "ground up" design do we need to build and test custom aspects?
- How much time/commitment do we need from you for design?

Delivery and Installation Elements:
- How long will it take?
- How long will our operation be down while the machine is being installed?
- How labor intensive will it be for us?

Maintenance Elements:
- How often does the machine break down?

- What are the service hours?
- How difficult will it be to train our team to run it?

Output Elements:

- How many units per hour will the machine put out?
- What is the supplier's machine's defect rate?
- Can the machine be run 24/7?

Upkeep Elements:

- What do maintenance costs look like in years two, three and four?
- How easily upgradeable is the machine?
- What is the machine's expected service life?

Terms and Conditions Elements:

- Should we lease vs. buy;
- Do we have flexibility of contracts;
- Do we offer payment terms; and
- What is the short-term product price.

In regard to design, you've determined that your alternative supplier does have a pretty good "off-the-shelf" machine, while your lead suppliers would require some customization. Their customization, however, would be free, and would require very little internal customer interface.

In terms of installation, your Engineering department has just found some independent studies showing that easily customizable machines— like those of your main supplier—are also relatively easy to install, and therefore end up taking about as much total time to install as less flexible "off-the-shelf" machines.

As far as maintenance is concerned, the folks in your Engineering department, and especially the engineer that just came over from the supplier, say your main supplier has a huge advantage in terms of their machine's reliability. Of course, we aren't likely to tell the supplier that, but it's one of their strengths.

With regard to output, the main supplier and their competitor are pretty close. Your alternative supplier's output may be a bit higher than your main supplier, but since the main supplier machines run a higher percentage of the time, it probably makes up for the difference.

In terms of upkeep, because of how they've been engineered, your main supplier machines break down much less frequently and, as a result, last longer.

Finally, in regard to terms and conditions, both offer lease or buy options. Your industry contracts are all pretty much the same and payment terms are usually 25 percent at signing, 25 percent on delivery and 50 percent when commissioned and running. Your main supplier's price is a bit higher, but you've determined that because of the reliability and flexibility of their machines, they have less downtime, easier long-term upgrades and longer shelf life. As a result, not only does your return on investment get better after year one, but their product is also less expensive to own in years two and three.

In answering the questions about each group of elements, you've determined that there is a value proposition gap between your main supplier and your alternatives in all but one of them. Based on that, you still feel good about this negotiation. You would prefer to reach agreement with the main supplier and you believe they would prefer you to replacing your business with several smaller customers at lower margins.

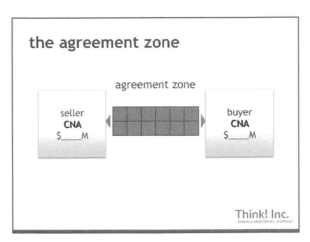

It's not unusual to see situations in which neither side has a clear idea of what they really want out of a negotiation beyond one or two simple items.

Trades

Trades are things of unequal value to you and your supplier. For example, providing an introduction to one of your company's other divisions may be of no cost to you, but will be of enormous value to your supplier. When things like this are added into the negotiation, they create opportunities to trade. So perhaps you could trade such an introduction for an additional one percent discount, and so on.

Why are trades important to us? It is much easier to divide a larger pie than a smaller one. It might just be the way we go from a five percent discount to eight percent without hurting supplier margins or our status as an ideal customer. Another important point about trades is that they typically are the same for the buyer or seller. What is different is the importance of those trades and the end of the range you desire.

Next, think through your organization's priorities. Your job is to identify things of value in your own organization and match as much as possible to your suppliers' prioritized goals. Trade for things of value to both sides in order to increase the size of the Agreement Zone and, ultimately, the deal.

CNA / trades impact on value
- value is measured relative to CNA
- trades help us add value to the deal and gain more for our own business

Think! Inc.
business negotiation, redefined

Trades are anything that could, and should, end up in writing, preferably in a contract. They must also be measurable. If you cannot measure it, you cannot trade it. Each trade should have a range that you have already defined internally. Ranges are like mini-Agreement Zones for each tradable item.

Trades need:

- A metric so we can measure
- A range to create the most flexibility we can
- A prioritization order
- An underlying interest to solve for (because while the supplier or internal customer may tell you WHAT they want, the true value lies in WHY they want it)

If we do not use trades, and focus only on price, our negotiation becomes a zero sum game with a winner and loser. Our deal is also likely to be less valuable to our own organization and to the long-term relationship with your supplier. There are well-documented stories of suppliers "winning" in a reverse auction, only to later go out of business or not be able to provide service because their margins were too small.

To achieve World Class levels in Procurement negotiation, we need to consider what our internal business stakeholders and multiple supplier stakeholders want and what is of value to them, and then add these things into the negotiations as trades. When this is done well, the value to our own organization increases substantially and our power with the seller organization grows. Buyers are no longer considered just price warriors, but instead, are viewed as business partners contributing to the overall value of the organization.

Never Concede, Always Trade

What precedent does it set when you concede to the supplier's demands during a negotiation? What message have you just sent the supplier when you concede? What precedent does it set when you demand concessions from a supplier? What messages have you sent them? There is a negotiation tactic called "nibbling," coming back to the negotiation and demanding a concession. This tactic has the effect of eroding trust and motivating both sides to "hold something back." Concessions are zero sum, they simply shift value from one party to the other. Trades on the other hand create value for one or both parties and are additive to a negotiation.

Instead of conceding, always trade for something. So if a supplier asks for something during a negotiation, your response should be, "There may be a pathway to that, if we trade for XXX [something you want]." To prepare for these inevitable conversations, be ready with some trades to offer that you know will be valuable to the supplier. You can develop these trades by doing your research in advance on the supplier's priorities, the industry issues and your past relationship with this supplier.

It helps to organize your supplier's thinking when you offer trades for them to consider. Suppliers don't often understand available trades, or they are bluffing. To clarify the supplier's priorities and what is important within their own organization, you need to get input from their stakeholders. Do not settle for just talking with the salesperson about a deal. You should try to Communicate with others in their organization who can identify what is important to them. Ask to visit their offices and speak with their executives and key stakeholders. Use these meetings as your opportunity to identify what is important and potentially tradable. Remember: good trade analysis is the best ammunition in gaining value and an overall better deal.

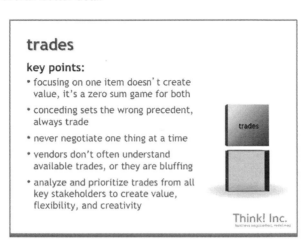

We often don't capture the true value of the deal because we don't view it through the eyes of the other side. For example, if Invoicing is an on-going issue for the supplier, then explore how electronic submission and payment could improve the process and be a valuable addition to the negotiation.

Many sellers continue to believe that buyers are only interested in low price. And buyers believe that sellers are always trying to increase their margin. But almost any business-to-business negotiation in which a professional buyer and seller are involved is likely to be a complex one with multiple criteria to be met on both sides, and buyers are certainly aware of that. Let's start by looking at the kind of analysis you need to do when dealing with suppliers.

The story is pretty much the same for "Wish List" (trade) items. Most professional buyers act on behalf of an internal customer and/or user group, and it's these individuals who help the buyer determine the trade items that will be negotiated in the deal. For example, someone sourcing technology for a production facility is likely to receive input from the vice president of Manufacturing, technicians on the manufacturing floor, and the vice president of Technology, as well as from people in other affected departments, such as Accounting. And those individuals are likely to want the buyer to concern themselves with price, length of contract, volume of purchase, which add-ons or value additions to purchase, warranty issues and support issues.

The point here is that professional buyers know what they want and are subject to even more pressure because they're acting on behalf of others. Given that, it only makes sense that in negotiating a deal you do all you can to achieve as many of your internal customer objectives as possible, and trading for items of importance.

Revenues, risk reduction and process improvements represent some of a typical supplier's stated needs but what underlying interests are driving them? It could be an impending IPO and the valuation of their firm, a change in regulatory process or desire to improve forecasting. There may be many more. You need to talk to suppliers using their language, helping them to understand how your trades address their underlying interests. Often times, when training buyers, we will ask, "Do you know what the supplier's Wish List is?" "Do you care?" The most common answer is "No" because buyers are so focused on what it is they want to achieve for their internal customers. In fact, you might be able to achieve even better results for your company by focusing on supplier desired trades that are high value and low cost.

Next, we trade for things that we want and that will provide additional value to us.

To satisfy underlying interests and create value, we trade items in and out of a deal that are valued differently by each side.

What might some of these tradable items be?

• Price/volume

• Length of contract, services

• Access to key decision makers

• Warranties

• Service

• Warehousing, shipping

• Payment terms

• Service Level Agreements (SLAs)

• Training and education

• Support

Trades have three levels:

• Level 1: Services and Products

• Level 2: Terms and Conditions

• Level 3: Creative/Strategic

While all levels of trades are important, Level 3 trades are more strategic and potentially more creative. Level 3 trades include things such as educational seminars, speaking engagements, access to key decision makers or innovation and technology that truly set the deal apart.

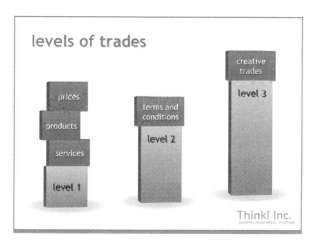

Level 1 and 2 are usually the easiest to include in deals, but make sure they are measurable. Level 3 is where the true differentiation can happen.

A few years ago, when a telecom company needed to upgrade some of their fleet vehicles, they decided it was also necessary to upgrade some options. In exchange for the upgrade, the company shared their fleet management and maintenance software with the vehicle broker, at no charge to the vehicle broker in exchange for more favorable pricing... a great Level 3 trade.

When an industrial engine manufacturer was experiencing damage on supplier deliveries of oversized and overweight parts, they worked with the supplier to make use of the engine manufacturer's in-house transportation carriers. The carriers were able to pick up the supplier parts at no additional charge and deliver them without damage.

How does trading combat price stalemates? Determining where to focus our efforts promotes deal creativity and inspiration. Trades are not concessions; they add value to one side or the other in exchange for something else. Our suppliers don't often practice this because their goals are predominantly to close deals and maximize their revenue. You may have to show them the pathway by adding trades to the deal.

Using the Blueprinting Process in a Large and Complex Negotiation

Let's return to this part of the process on a "live deal" involving thorough analysis around the second aspect of the negotiation blueprint: trades.

As you recall, it's April 1st and you're preparing to communicate to your preferred supplier that after all your months of trying to get to closure on buying some of their machines, it's finally down to a choice between them and your CNA (i.e., their competitor). Before you issue this formal challenge, you complete step two: trade analysis.

Step One: Trade Analysis for You and Your Supplier

You complete an overview of your Wish List of trades in the event you and the supplier desire to move forward after CNA analysis. Recall that CNA determines if a business arrangement provides value to both sides (the Agreement Zone). Now, it's time to determine what they will accept, what you will pay and how risk will be shared in exchange for that value.

Step Two: Wish List of Trades—Our Side

You've pulled together your same internal team and someone from the Legal department for this estimation and, after much wrangling, have prioritized your Wish List of trades as follows:

Wish List Estimation Our Side

Rank	Item	Weight	Range ("preferred" to "will accept")
1	Price	40%	$200k – $250K per machine
2	Ongoing service	25%	24 x 7 – 8 x 5
3	Upgrades	15%	Free – 75% discount
4	Length of contract	10%	1 year – ??
5	Volume	5%	2 machines – ??
6	Man hours you provide for installation	5%	200–100

Step Three: Wish List of Trades—The Supplier's Side

With the help of the engineer who used to work for your supplier, you've estimated the types of trades this supplier has looked for in the past and come up with the following educated guesses for the supplier's Wish List:

Wish List Estimation Supplier's Side

Rank	Item	Weight	Range ("preferred" to "will accept")
1	Length of contract	30%	3–1 years
2	Price	25%	$300k – $250k per machine
3	Volume	15%	3–2 machines
4	Upgrades	15%	50% discount – free
5	Man hours you provide for installation	10%	100–150
6	On-going service	5%	8 x 5 – 24 x 7

Summary on Primary Uses for Blueprinting CNA and Trade Analysis

1. Make better, higher value decisions on supplier selection

2. Make better decisions on price and risk to acquire that value

3. Capture more of the value for our side and achieve maximum savings for us

4. Effective planning and management of the negotiation process and tactics
5. Preparing and responding to offers

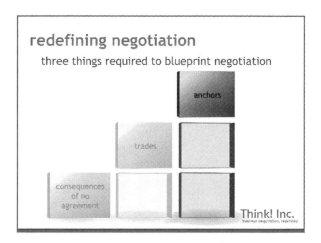

Anchors

We have focused on what we are competing against (their CNA) and how we can create value in the deal (trading items of differing value). Now we will focus on the third key component to blueprint negotiations: anchors. Anchors are the primary factor affecting how the value we have created is divided between you and the supplier.

Anchors influence a buyer's or seller's thinking because they establish points in the negotiation that tend to make the value of the deal lean toward one side or another.

When a supplier tries to anchor a deal it can delay and confuse the deal if it is not reflective of accurate and good data, or not within the defined Agreement Zone.

Anchors are very useful for buyers when we use them on the offensive, and can back them up with solid data. If we anchor a deal by establishing a price within the Agreement Zone that captures most of the value for our side, we are likely to complete the negotiation close to this anchor point.

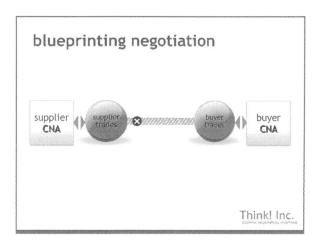

We use CNAs, trades and anchors to blueprint and execute our overall negotiation. By using these three components, we can conceptualize the negotiation. Much like building a new house, we need the overall outline (blueprint) to understand how it will be built to our satisfaction, including how the rooms are arranged, how many bathrooms are included, what the kitchen will look like, etc. In professional buying negotiations, blueprinting is essential to manage the overall process.

We know from data collected over 16 years that there is a relatively small variance in opening price and structure (anchor) and closing price/structure. We often say if we anchor on "it" we are most likely going to end up negotiating "it." For example, if we want the negotiation to be simply about price, then structuring our opening offer on price only will suffice. If it's a more complex negotiation where other things such as price, terms, SLAs, indemnification and a total value-based solution are important, then we need to re-think the strategic use of anchors. We want to change the conversation through strategic and thoughtful anchoring.

When we refer to structure in an opening offer, we are referring to the "branding" of the negotiation. Do we want to negotiate the price of engineering services or the quality output of those services?

An anchor has more impact on the final outcome of how the value gets created and divided than anything else that happens in a negotiation.

Anchors take many forms:

- An opening offer
- An RFP
- Suppliers marketing piece or price list
- Last year's deal
- The way the industry structures deals
- The desire of one internal stakeholder

Who Should Open First to Anchor the Deal?

Let's start with the most obvious anchor, the opening offer. How do you feel about opening first? Many buyers have been taught never to open with the first offer or to make such an unreasonably low offer that it will catch the supplier off guard. Is this a good idea? In situations where we have little data on both sides' CNAs and trades, no, it is not a good idea because any unreasonable offer outside the Agreement Zone will simply not be acceptable and will delay the negotiation. But if we have done a good job of defining the CNAs and trades for both sides we know where to anchor in order to capture the most value for us and still be a good deal for the supplier.

There is no one correct answer. However, we feel that the buyer should always open first because if you let the other side open first, then you are letting them anchor the negotiation. Open with your anchor as close to the supplier's CNA as possible. This means your initial offer should be as low as possible, but staying within the Agreement Zone. If you go beyond the supplier's CNA and outside the Agreement Zone, the supplier's alternatives look more appealing and they will walk away.

To anchor the negotiation that creates and captures the most value, you will need to know the CNAs of both sides in order to place an effective opening offer within the Agreement Zone. You should anchor the negotiation marginally better than their alternative because we know that the final offer will not move far from the opening offer. As a result, you claim the majority of the value in the deal and more cost savings.

Anchors are the way to change the conversation, focus on what a good deal means to both sides and drive acquisition price down.

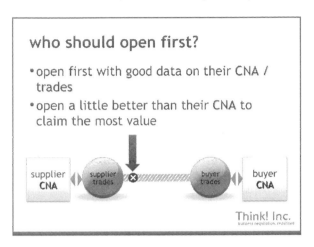

By opening with an initial offer that is marginally better than their alternative, we have immediately placed additional real value on the table. You will be perceived as trustworthy and credible by the other side because the deal is within the acceptable Agreement Zone.

Have you ever made an initial offer without knowing the other side's alternative and what a great deal looks like for them? When you do that you may be leaving money on the table. Or perhaps you anchored way too low, out of the Agreement Zone, and thus you erode trust with the supplier.

We want to open marginally better than the supplier's CNA in order to claim the most value.

Unreasonable Anchors

Sometimes the supplier puts out unreasonable anchors.

How should you deal with unreasonable anchors made by the other side? *Simply ignore them*. Do not counter their offer. You do not have to answer just because they ask! For example, if you have a target acquisition price of $100 per item, and the supplier anchors with an offer of $190, simply ignore it. Come back with the lowest offer that is still above their CNA and you set the anchor in order to change the conversation and capture a better deal. By simply re-anchoring you will end up with a better deal.

When the other side makes an initial offer that you believe is unreasonable or poorly frames the overall negotiation, you should not respond to it. Instead, ask questions to re-anchor the deal.

The best response is to ignore the anchor, ask questions about the offer and then give your own anchor to capture more of the value.

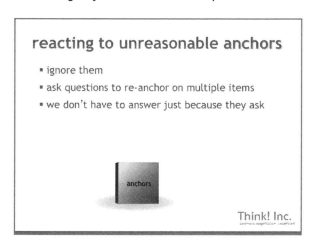

Verbal Tactics as Anchors

Your supplier may try all kinds of tactics to get a deal closed, such as trying to go around the formal procurement process or putting pressure on timelines. For any negotiating tactic, we can use Think! Inc. tools to determine our response and bring the negotiation process back on track.

Executives and politicians who get PR training are a good example of using tools. They are not taught to memorize certain responses when asked tough questions, or anticipate all possible questions. Instead, they are taught to categorize the questions in subject headings, to then formulate a response according to the heading, and finally, to use their own style to respond to the question. This is a much more organic and authentic way of responding rather than memorizing 20 plus canned statements or checklists of items offered in other negotiations training.

Use of Tactics

One of the reasons the Value Blueprint is so important is that virtually all of the dialogue between you and your internal customers and the supplier flows through it. We studied verbal negotiating tactics between buyer and seller in 19 countries for two years and 97 percent of them fell into two categories:

1. Reference to alternatives (CNA)
2. Request for concession (trades)

Both buyers and sellers will use tactics and specific language to advance their own goals in a negotiation. Some of these tactics include:

Buyer Trade Tactics:

- *"Lower your price"*
- *"It's not in my budget"*

Buyer CNA Tactics:

- *"The competition has better service"*
- *"I can do this in-house"*

Combined CNA and Trade Tactics:

- *"I can get the same thing from someone else cheaper"*
- *"Everyone else gives that away for free"*

Seller Trade Tactics:

- *"I need to increase my price"*
- *"That price is below our cost"*

Seller CNA Tactics:

- *"Other customers pay more"*
- *"We're running at full capacity"*

Combined CNA and Trade Tactics:

- *"I can sell the same thing somewhere else for more"*
- *"All of our other customers pay for service"*

The more we know about both sides' alternatives and all the items we wish to trade, the more we can either challenge these items or bring them back into context. When a supplier says, "I can sell that for higher rates or easily replace you." If we have data on their CNA and trades, we can counter that tactic. Many times the real problem is that there might be 20 criteria in the CNA for the supplier and they will choose the one aspect where they, in fact, have a better alternative to us. It is then important to be able to bring the discussion back into context. For example, they may indeed have a customer that will pay more but you might be more financially stable, growing faster or have more divisions that they can grow into.

How do your suppliers anchor you? Pricing? Timing? Quantity? If the supplier gives you a price, is that really their best price? Most of the time it is not. If any of these things change your behavior, you have been anchored!

Buyers often focus on only one thing: price. But in the best strategic negotiations, professional buyers get more of what they want and what their stakeholders want by adding and dividing value through trades. Bundle other things into your negotiation to change the conversation from price to overall deal value and you will be well on your way to improved deals.

Managing Uncertainty

There will always be some level of uncertainty about the other side's CNA and trades. Even the most seasoned and experienced buyers have trouble getting perfect data.

Given all of the uncertainty surrounding the structure of the deal for the other side, and yet, given the consequences to our side if we are wrong or do not capture the most value in the deal, does it make sense to put only one offer on the table? We put suppliers in a "take it or leave it" situation with one offer, precisely what we are trying to avoid in order to capture the most value for our side.

Now we are going to introduce the last concept of Strategic Negotiation that will tie all of our other concepts together and give you the highest probability of success.

Multiple Equal Offers (MEOs)

Multiple Equal Offers (MEOs) give us the most flexibility in presenting offers. They allow us to keep in control, solicit additional information from the supplier and often act as a good diffuser for any potential conflict in negotiation.

MEOs are two or more business solutions—approximately equal in value to us, but representing different value propositions to the supplier. We would be prepared to accept any of our MEOs if the supplier agreed.

We believe that the offers are of variable value to the other side because the way we bundle various trades in each offer represents a variance in value to the other side. We place these offers on the table and ask the other side, "Which of these approaches/solutions do you find most desirable?" Even if they don't choose one, this approach ends up acting as a sensitivity analysis to multiple needs and opens up the dialogue to creative solutions.

MEOs can be used internally as well. When you have multiple stakeholders with multiple needs, these different solution options can be shown internally first so that your stakeholders see their needs in relation to the needs of others in the organization. Presenting MEOs to your internal stakeholders will give everyone an opportunity to evaluate the alternatives and their own priorities.

MEOs in RFPs

We also recommend using MEOs in the RFP process. Add a few paragraphs to the RFP suggesting that your supplier provide alternative deals as part of their offers. Or, provide some suggested MEOs that fit with your desired deal outcome. Ask the RFP suppliers to respond to these. Opening RFPs to creative responses may introduce some new ideas you hadn't thought of and will likely increase the overall value to your company.

It is important to title each MEO, as you do not want the other side guessing what you are trying to accomplish. The title should clarify your intent for each alternative. Descriptive titles such as "Basic Value" or "Focus on Future Growth" or "Greatest Flexibility" will help to communicate your intent.

MEOs are all custom built, not "off-the-shelf," and include Level 1, 2 and 3 trades.

Sensitivity Analysis

MEOs help to reduce uncertainty in the deal and allow for sensitivity analysis because they provide an opportunity for your supplier to react and discuss their priorities with you. MEOs result in a sensitivity analysis from the supplier (e.g., if you place 3 alternative offers in front of your supplier, you will hear what they like or what they don't like). This is the intention, to continue to have suppliers offer data and dialogue, and to help them focus on what they really want.

MEOs help to avoid value-dividing concessions by showing the other side that we are flexible and prepared to consider alternative approaches. However, these alternative approaches do not contain just one item or issue. MEOs contain multiple tradable items.

We populate the MEOs based on the potential trades identified in our trade analysis of our own internal stakeholders and of their issues and priorities.

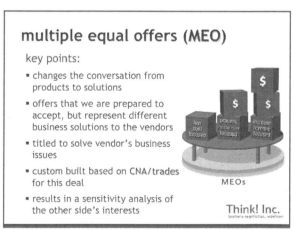

How does the use of MEOs change the conversation with our suppliers? When we present MEOs, our likelihood of higher value and lower Total Cost of Ownership (TCO) improves. It would be easy to focus on our issues and what we want out of a deal, but then the negotiation would drag on, as the supplier would try to put together a reasonable response for their side. Why not start with three reasonable alternative offers, which you already know are in the Agreement Zone, signaling that you are serious about getting a deal done?

Have you purchased a computer or tablet or iPod lately? If so, you were probably asked how much memory you wanted, if you needed a case, what color, what phone service, etc. You could have just walked away with the lowest-level device with no accessories and very little memory, but most people do not buy this way. You probably spent some time putting together a bundle that was just right for you.

MEOs are a lot like that—everyone leaves with a product, but it doesn't necessarily have to be filled with the same memory or be the same color. In essence, MEOs give suppliers three choices for closing a deal instead of just one.

MEO example

Invest and Create Value: Build long-term relationship	Grow the Relationship: Explore areas of mutual value	Maintain Partnership: Process excellence
Contract Term: 3 years	Contract Term: 2 years	Contract Term: 1 year
Payment: 2/10 N30	Payment: Net 30 days	Payment: Net 45 days
Minimum volume commitment: 100% to total need	Minimum commitment: 75% of total need	Business Reviews: Semi-annual
Volume rebate: 3%	Dedicated customer response team	
Intro to other operating units(s)	Business reviews: Quarterly	
Business reviews: Quarterly		

Think! Inc.
business negotiation, redefined

Let's return to the part of the process on a "live deal" involving the development of MEOs.

Step 3 of Our "Live Deal" Case Study: MEOs

You tell them that based on both sides' needs and the value proposition of their competitor, you've put together three different relationships that you highlight on a flipchart or PowerPoint presentation. You briefly overview some key elements of each, then offer everyone a handout containing the details and go through them. You now ask them to rank the three offers in terms of their preference. They quickly agree that the short-term option is the least preferable, but there's a lot of internal negotiation among them over which of the remaining options are most preferable. It's obvious that neither is quite right, so at this point you begin the trading to come up with one solution that fits their needs. You keep going back to total costs. They try to push you for concessions; you continue to trade using both Wish Lists.

Trade	Long-term Partnership	Transactional Relationship	Short
Length	3 years	One machine at a time	1 year
Price	$225k / machine	$245k	$235
Volume	3 machines	1	2
Service	5 days x 24 hours	Pay per service	7x24
Upgrades	25% discount	At current market rates when needed	30%
Support	300 hours	100	200

In the end, you settle on this deal:

FINAL AGREEMENT: Long-Term Partnership
Length: Three years
Price: $255K per machine
Volume: Three machines
Service: Five days x 24 hours
Upgrades: 25% discount
Installation Support: 300 hours

How Is Value Measured?

Value is measured relative to each side's CNAs. It is this incremental value that the other side realizes, that causes them to want to do a deal.

For example, what is bottled water worth to you if it is available in your company break room? Or down the street at a convenience store? Or at the airport waiting for a flight? Or during 100-degree weather at Walt Disney World with your children as you are standing in the one-hour wraparound line to Splash Mountain? Different value? Yes. Value is measured relative to your CNA.

The critical aspect of value is that it is not measured equally by each side. Value is two-dimensional. The difference in perceived value of a particular tradable item defines the value it creates in the business deal. This is why we title each alternative MEO and bundle trades—to represent varying values to the buyer and seller.

When there are gaps in our knowledge of the supplier's CNA, we can use MEOs to test those gaps. If a supplier responds to an MEO with more information about his company's preferences and priorities, you are clarifying the supplier's CNA. From the discussion you have with your supplier about alternative bundles, you can also define more trades and develop additional MEOs.

How do we determine what makes a great deal? By considering all of the elements that create value in the deal. These are trades/tradable items that make up our MEOs. First we need to make sure that on average we meet or beat their overall CNA. Same goes for us.

Blueprinting the Negotiation

Throughout the process of Strategic Negotiation, you are working on the overall blueprint of the deal. In our workshops, we use a pre-populated software tool to dispense and capture information as you move through the process. Included in this tool is information discovered and researched about each side's CNAs, priorities and trades and finally, MEOs. These things comprise the structural drawing or blueprint of the deal.

The goals we prescribe for negotiation are to create joint value and to divide that value given concerns for fairness in the ongoing relation-ship. In other words, if you're going to be working with this supplier in the future, be sure that both sides consider the results to be a "good deal."

45

Case Studies

We have added case studies to this book to help you understand how the concepts of Strategic Negotiation and the Think! Inc. methodology apply in buying situations. While the cases are based on our real experiences, the stories have been fictionalized and are not meant to describe any particular person or company. The cases have been organized by industry and topic so you can view those most relevant to your situation.

Part 2: Case Studies

Case Studies

Case	Industry	Topic
1. Home Advantage Stores *"A Growing Problem"*	Retail	Solving for the true problem, outsourcing
2. BevSure and Aqua Co *"A Surly Attitude"*	Industrial Products	Beyond just price
3. Falcon Theaters *"3-way Solution"*	Entertainment	Adding partners to deals
4. Oil and Pipefitting Company: Part 1 *"Bankrupt!"*	Oil and Gas	Negotiating in bankruptcy
5. Oil and Pipefitting Company: Part 2 *"Customers Affect Procurement"*	Oil and Gas	How your customers can affect your deals
6. Baumans Co. & Premier Works *"Aggregating Demand"*	Marketing Trade Shows and Electronics	Aggregating demand
7. Pershing Auto Parts & Value Electric *"Disaster Happens"*	Automotive	Failed negotiations
8. Universal Electronics Smart Phone Cameras *"A Picture's Worth a Thousand Words"*	Consumer Electronics	Creative and strategic trades for a critical supplier
9. Wright Agriculture Company *"International Single Source Negotiations Germany and China"*	Farm and Garden Equipment	International single source negotiations

Case Study #1 – The Home Advantage Stores

"A Growing Problem"

Situation Overview and Business Problem

Morgan Samuels, the Regional Manager of 28 Home Advantage stores in the southeastern U.S., was in a quandary. His home improvement retail stores boasted the largest Garden Centers in the region (far larger than his competitors) but lately, the Centers' flowers and other living plants were inexplicably dying or were looking less than optimally healthy.

Home Advantage provided and sold do-it-yourself home construction products like tools, lumber, home appliances and gardening supplies. Gardening was enormously popular throughout the southeastern U.S. and in the past, the Home Advantage Garden Centers were very profitable, providing some of the highest margins in the stores. To keep customers interested and in support of the Garden Centers' growing popularity and profits, Home Advantage spent a disproportionate part of the advertising budget on Garden Center ads.

A Dying Problem

With the recent problem of dying plants, customers were starting to complain and were taking their business elsewhere. The last time Morgan visited one of the stores in North Carolina, he ordered the store manager and the purchasing manager to "get this situation fixed." The spoilage rate for the plants, as well as the cost to maintain them, was beginning to escalate. Plants were dying in the Garden Centers before they could be sold to customers, and with Home Advantage product guarantees, the stores were seeing a lot of customers coming back for refunds.

The North Carolina store manager didn't know what to do and was very concerned that his job might be at stake if he didn't resolve this issue immediately. The Regional Purchasing Manager for garden products, Betty So, informed him that Home Advantage's two-year contract with its regional supplier, a wholesale plant grower called Green Gardens, was soon coming to an end. Betty explained that this created two options: renegotiate their contract or select a new supplier for the Garden Centers.

Betty had overall responsibility for the Green Gardens relationship and over the past three months she had had many meetings with them to discuss Home Advantage's plant problem. She had also been meeting with several potential new suppliers, just in case they had to end their contract with Green Gardens. Green Gardens didn't have any solutions for Home Advantage's plant problem; they insisted that they were delivering healthy plants every week. Furthermore, they claimed that Home Advantage must be abusing or mistreating the plants in some way and suggested that Betty investigate.

Alternative Suppliers

The other potential suppliers that Betty was in talks with were keenly interested and guaranteed they would be able to deliver healthy plants. The main problem with selecting a new supplier was the cost to get them up and running (including changing out all the current stock, developing the packaging, integrating their systems with Home Advantage systems, etc). Betty dreaded having to switch suppliers because it required so much time and attention. Bringing new vendors up to Home Advantage's standards was estimated to cost over $100,000 and she knew this had to be included in the total cost calculations. In addition to that, Home Advantage was on a 90-day pay cycle. New vendors always complained about this and tried to negotiate better terms, while Green Gardens was used to it. Changing vendors represented a lot of hard, extra work for Betty, who was barely keeping up with her normal workload.

Betty was so busy buying all kinds of things for the region that she really didn't have any time to try to solve these kinds of problems. If she wasted time trying to address the Green Gardens issues or bring up a new vendor, she wouldn't be able to complete her daily workload and achieve her performance goals each month, which were tied to her annual bonus.

Tough Alternatives

Joel Jarvis, the store manager for the North Carolina store, was under great pressure from the Regional Manager to fix the plant situation, and he felt the need to share this pressure with Betty. After a lengthy discussion about the problem and the options, the situation boiled down to two potential solutions:

1. Sales had to improve and the margins of the Garden Center products had to recover (which was highly unlikely but there was always hope of a miracle!).

2. Betty would have to get a price reduction of 10–15 percent from Green Gardens, which would have the same profitability results, at least in the short-term.

In the long-term, Joel knew that more and more customers would go elsewhere for their garden goods if the plants at Home Advantage weren't healthy. That would also have an effect on all garden supplies sales where the margins were even higher, averaging 30–40 percent. Most of the other supplies, such as pots, garden tools and garden equipment, were sourced in China, as were most of the products sold throughout Home Advantage. The only way Home Advantage could stay in business and compete against other home improvement stores was to keep the cost of goods sold (COGS) very low through China sourcing and to attract customers by having a thriving Garden Center.

The plants had to be sourced locally or regionally because of climate-specific varieties. Betty just didn't see how to get Green Gardens to reduce their price. The alternative of going to another vendor wasn't very attractive either because of the associated cost and workload. A thought crossed Betty's mind about Home Advantage competitors and what they were doing about their Garden Centers, but with all of her regular daily tasks, she really didn't have time to investigate that.

Garden Center Inventory

Before contacting Green Gardens again, Betty tried to think of any reasons why the plants were quickly spoiling. She approached the Garden Center manager, Jose Ramirez, in the lunchroom last week, but he was too busy to chat as Joel had asked him to take over the management of the plumbing department in addition to the Garden Centers. Jose assured Betty that his employees were careful to water the plants every day and to make sure that they were getting enough sunlight.

But the plants are still inexplicably dying…, Betty thought.

Jose was very aware of how the Garden Centers' poor products were affecting sales, so he did not want to risk Betty buying and receiving more plants that were going to be left on the shelves to eventually die. One of Jose's performance goals was to improve inventory turns and his bonus was tied to this. Jose had asked Betty to minimize the plant buys until spring.

– – –

Spring started a few weeks later and Home Advantage still had no acceptable solutions. Joel was frustrated with Betty's lack of progress and Betty was at her wits end. These were the months where the Garden Centers' plants should have been thriving; they were also the peak months for plant sales but the unhealthy plants were just driving away more customers. Joel really started pressuring Betty to get Green Gardens to reduce their price by 15 percent for the next two-year contract. Betty did not want to end the business relationship with Green Gardens, but at this point, she saw no other choice if Green Gardens refused the price reduction. The quality of the Garden Centers' customer service was also suffering since the employees could not explain to customers why their plants were not up to par.

The Cost Reduction Demand

Being left with the ultimate decision of getting the supplier to lower the cost or go to a new vendor, Betty called Green Gardens to schedule a meeting. With the weight and pressure of lowering costs upon her shoulders, Betty skipped right to the point during the meeting and demanded a 15 percent price reduction for their renewed two-year contract. Green Gardens pushed back hard, explaining they were delivering plants on time and in healthy condition. Tom Rauch, the President of Green Gardens, became angry and accused Home Advantage of mishandling the plants.

"We have plenty of records that the plants were delivered in healthy condition to Home Advantage and other home improvement stores in the area," he said. "We don't experience these problems with your competitors," he said.

The meeting ended with no resolution and a lot of tension between Green Gardens and Home Advantage.

Investigating and Validating the Problem

After this frustrating meeting that resolved nothing, Betty decided that the time had come to investigate the situation more closely. She spent a day working in one of Home Advantage's 28 Garden Centers with Jose's employees. She observed the employees assisting customers and asked a lot of questions about the general maintenance of the Garden Center.

"What do you know about these flowers?"

"How much water/sun do they need and how often?"

"Are these indoor or outdoor plants?"

She thought that most of her questions were very basic and general but after receiving vague responses from the Garden Center employees, she realized that they were not very knowledgeable about the plants. Some of them even frankly told her that they did not know much about plants and didn't really care as they specialized more in plumbing or lumber. They were just picking up the slack from the recently shorted staff.

When Jose came by the Center after lunch to check up on how things were going, Betty asked him some of the same questions she had been asking his employees. She received the same vague responses. For example, when she asked him how often the plants needed to be watered, Jose stated matter-of-factly, "I don't know...we water all the plants every day, sometimes three times a day." A customer overheard the tail-end of their conversation and voiced surprise to hear that the Garden Center was watering the plants so often.

"Clearly, you guys are over-watering!" the customer exclaimed.

After this incident, Betty did a little online research on the care of the kinds of plants in the Garden Centers. She found out that some plants that should be in the sun were being housed in the shade and vice versa, some plants did not need to be watered every day, etc. A quick call to Green Gardens to ask about the proper care of the plants confirmed Betty's research results.

A Different Approach

Betty sat and mulled over her newfound information. Her day in the Garden Center had revealed that the employees working there were not properly trained, were not knowledgeable about plant care and, in some cases, weren't interested in learning. This resulted in improper care of the plants, which ultimately led to the plants' rising spoilage rate. What could she do with this information? What solution would benefit both Home Advantage and Green Gardens? Maybe she was focusing on the wrong goal, she thought. Perhaps demanding a price reduction was not the best approach.

She thought about asking Green Gardens if they would consider training the Centers' employees, or perhaps even taking over the Garden Centers as an outsourced service provider. These were certainly different approaches to solving the problem. Betty favored outsourcing as a solution because she believed this would reduce the overall cost to Home Advantage. She would have to work with Accounting and HR to verify the cost-savings numbers in employees, space, etc. Through outsourcing, the Garden Centers would get professionally trained, knowledgeable and passionate employees, and the stores would not have to invest time and money to train their current employees. The current Home Advantage Garden Center staff could be reassigned to other areas of the store or could choose to stay in the Garden Centers as employees of Green Gardens.

Betty felt pretty good about these creative alternatives. She was considering a broader solution and a more strategic one.

Betty called Tom Rauch to propose her initial idea of outsourcing Garden Center staff. She was happy to hear that he was open to discussing the alternatives.

Consequences of No Agreement (CNAs)

Betty had been collecting data on Green Gardens over several months and was sure they had mentioned some strategic information at a few meetings. She went back to her meeting notes to analyze how she could apply the Strategic Negotiation process to her situation.

She estimated what would happen if she and her supplier did not reach an agreement. Betty had learned from the Strategic Negotiation workshop that the purpose of estimating the "Consequences of No Agreement" (CNAs) was to enable her to determine what effects—positive and negative—of not reaching an agreement would have on both the buyer and seller.[4] Estimating the CNAs would help Betty determine the impact that the consequences would have on both sides, as well as the extent to which they would make any potential deal attractive or not attractive.[5] Furthermore, it would help her understand who had the true power in the negotiation process.

Buyer's side. Betty needed to validate that the Home Advantage solution for every proposed alternative deal would be better than her alternatives and better than every one of Green Gardens' alternatives. She recognized that if they did not reach an agreement with Green Gardens, they could end their contract. Home Advantage's consequences would then be to go to a new vendor at the estimated cost of $100,000, which included many hard and soft costs and a huge amount of time and effort. They would have to build a new relationship with a new company, begin a new contract, become familiar with their policies, procedures, and staff, negotiate pricing, etc. And all this would happen during the peak Spring selling season.

- Transition to another supplier = $100,000
- Potential cost savings = $0
- Reduced or loss of sales due to dying plants = $70,000
- Reduced customer satisfaction—potential loss of business to competitors = $5 million

Seller's side. Green Gardens simply could not afford to lose Home Advantage. Although Green Gardens provided many different types of

---

[4] Brian J. Dietmeyer with Rob Kaplan, *Strategic Negotiation*, 44.

[5] Ibid., 45.

plants to a variety of Garden Centers throughout the United States, Home Advantage was by far their largest customer, representing approximately 45 percent of their annual revenue. If they lost Home Advantage as a client, Green Gardens would have to subsequently conduct lay-offs to save costs and might ultimately become unprofitable for the first time in their company history.

- Loss of 15 percent profit = $1.5 million
- Competitor empowerment—loss of additional business to competitor because of damaged reputation = $3 million
- Loss of growing/farming volume (costs will increase)
  - Short-term = $80,000
  - Long-term = $2 million
- Loss of major customer (soft costs)
  - Loss of key reference
  - Loss of grower volume
  - Employee lay-offs

Identifying Anchors

Armed with the CNAs for both Home Advantage and Green Gardens, Betty and her manager were ready for their next face-to-face meeting with Green Gardens to confirm their estimations and further discuss the options. In addition to confirming the CNAs, Betty wanted this meeting to serve as a platform for her to anchor the deal on price. She was determined to squeeze some savings out of this deal as well as improve the service for the Garden Center. The Strategic Negotiation workshop had taught her that there were two types of anchors—opening offers and other items. She learned that anchors have a significant impact on negotiation outcomes. Being the first to anchor the deal would, ultimately, get her a bigger portion of the pie.[6]

Betty had also learned that anchors are not limited to just price.

---

[6] Ibid., 112–113.

In fact, it was never quite that simple and it was always good to think of other anchors that might be offered, such as timing of the deal. She had planned to provide an opening offer of the initial 15 percent price reduction. This, she calculated, would be an acceptable offer for both sides, although better for her.[7]

During the meeting with Green Gardens, Betty and Joel confirmed their CNAs estimations. Home Advantage was, in fact, Green Gardens' largest client and they clearly did not want to lose the business. After discussing Betty's opening offer of the 15 percent price reduction, Betty asked Green Gardens to take a tour of Home Advantage's Garden Centers to investigate the problem themselves in an attempt to better understand the situation and come up with a resolution. Green Gardens agreed.

Identifying and Dividing Value

The COO of Green Gardens and Tom Rauch accompanied Betty and Joel on the Home Advantage Garden Center tour. During the tour, it was obvious that the Garden Centers' employees were very inexperienced and mostly uninterested in gardening. They didn't know how to best take care of the plants. Green Gardens confirmed their suspicions that that was the underlying problem.

Betty and Joel admitted that improper plant care was part of the problem, but it didn't change the fact that they still needed the price reduction. After some thought, Tom told them that Green Gardens used a database that identified which plants were appropriate for each micro-climate in the region. This database specifically explained how to care for each plant and, most importantly, which plants were the best and most popular sellers in each geographic region. Tom thought that this might help Home Advantage design an approach for featuring the most profitable and highest volume sellers. He asked if access to this database would benefit Home Advantage.

"Definitely!" Betty proclaimed.

In light of this new information, Green Gardens then proposed that

---

[7] Ibid., 14.

they meet again later in the week to discuss the next step.

In the meantime, Betty and Joel went back to their CNA estimations to see if they could create additional measurable business value[8] for both sides. This way, they could decide what was most important to them in the deal, which, in turn, would determine how they might effectively divide value and trade different elements of the deal with Green Gardens. Betty was starting to enjoy this process and Joel was feeling optimistic about a deal that would improve the situation. They came up with the following potential trades:

Home Advantage's potential trades:

- Price concessions (they might be willing to pay more if sales increased) of two to 10 percent more
- Outsourcing Garden Center operations—savings of $129–$159K per store
- Introduction to other Regional Home Advantage operations—no cost to HA
- Joint advertising—savings of $75K per year if GG pitched in half of the budget
- References—no cost to HA
- Addition of an indoor house plant section in another area of the store, near the check-outs—potential new revenue stream of $100K per year
- Addition of a cut flowers section near the check-outs—potential new revenue stream of $100K per year
- Longer contract terms – no cost to HA

Green Garden's potential trades:

- Price concessions—discount of zero to five percent if absolutely necessary

---

[8] Ibid., 21.

- Longer contract terms (three plus years) with HA, resulting in better strategic planning at company-owned farms to meet peak demand
- Development of special hybrids for the region—little additional cost to GG
- Training of employees on the care of plants—200–300 employees across the region
- Access to plant database for care of plants—no cost to GG
- Access to plant database for best sellers and trending information—no cost to GG
- Phone or in-person support from Green Gardens $75–$80K per year

Identifying Multiple Equal Offers (MEOs)

After the meeting and Garden Center tour, Betty and Joel worked on three different equivalent offers for Green Gardens. These offers were developed using the information gathered over several months, including the meeting and tour the previous week. Betty felt they had solid, useful information and could develop a few alternative offers that would be acceptable to both Home Advantage and Green Gardens. Betty had learned that the point of these options, called Multiple Equal Offers (MEOs), was that they were all acceptable to Home Advantage, but of varying value to Green Gardens. This meant that they could trade for things that were of little cost to Home Advantage, but of high value to Green Gardens, such as special advertising. Green Gardens could give access to their best-selling database at little cost to them, but at high value to Home Advantage. These were just the kinds of trades that made sense and added significant value to the overall deal. Adding in the trades made the overall contract worth roughly $10 million over two years (up from the current $2.3 million contract). These MEOs also promised to solve the spoilage problem as well as free up some Home Advantage employees for assignments to other departments.

Joel and Betty called their Regional Manager, Morgan, to inform him of the progress. "These MEOs create and divide value that ultimately form a better solution," Betty and Joel explained to Morgan. "The table [below] details the MEOs we have developed," she said. "Each option has several elements: price, length of contract and other trades. These additional trades will increase the overall value of the deal and will bring more value and greater sales to Home Advantage."

MEOs

Item	Outsourcing	Blue Support	Green Support
Price change	10% increase cost to Home Advantage	15% discount for Home Advantage	0% discount
Plant Life Guarantee	90 days	7 days	30 days
Contract length	5 years	1 year	2 years
Access to plant database	Yes	Yes	Yes
Support	Outsourced staff – Green Gardens runs the Center	3 days/week phone support	• 5 days/week on-site training and support • Information on plant care included with each shipment
Add Indoor Plants and Cut Flowers	Yes	No	• Limited
Special Advertising	Yes	No	• Some

Negotiation Results

Feeling good about the MEOs that they came up with, Betty and Joel arranged their next meeting to present these offers to Green Gardens. Morgan asked to join them. Green Gardens was extremely interested in the Outsourcing option as it applied to all 28 regional stores. They would also increase their revenue with a longer contract. Home

Advantage benefited from this option as well, since they would cut staff costs through outsourcing, gain access to Green Gardens' plant database and be able to sell additional high-margin products (indoor plants and bouquets).

Both sides also came to an agreement on quarterly Key Performance Indicators (KPIs) to drive at least a 20 percent increase in Garden Center sales and a six percent increase through the addition of indoor plants and bouquets.

Although Home Advantage initially began with an ultimate negotiation goal of reducing the contract price by 10 to 15 percent, they ended up with a solution that was more valuable to both themselves and Green Gardens. Home Advantage expected to increase overall Garden Center sales by 26 percent. In addition, they could reduce costs through outsourcing some employees, while at the same time improving overall customer satisfaction. Morgan and Joel also believed that with an improved Garden Center, overall traffic and sales from other sections of the stores would also improve.

Epilogue

Once Home Advantage and Green Gardens reached a detailed agreement and got their contract approved by the Legal department, they were ready to begin the process of outsourcing Home Advantage's Garden Center staff. Green Gardens assigned a project manager for each of the 28 Home Advantage stores to assure a smooth transition.

Morgan, Joel and Betty marked Green Gardens' first day running the Home Advantage Garden Center with a ribbon-cutting ceremony.

Lessons Learned

Betty leveraged what she had learned about Strategic Negotiation to achieve a more valuable deal. In this case, they learned that collecting data on the vendor and having open communication was key. Betty and Joel were able to estimate, identify and confirm their CNAs based on the information that they had about Green Gardens. This led to creating value for both sides, and developing options (MEOs) that were equally valuable to Betty and Joel but of varying value to Green Gardens. In short, they learned that the elements of the Strategic Negotiation methodology led to greater mutual success.

Case Study #2 – BevSure and Aqua Co

"A Surly Attitude"

Situation Overview and Business Problem

The air at the BevSure weekly staff meeting with the Procurement department was stiff and cold. The company's contract with Aqua Company (Aqua Co), an organization that provided sustainability solutions for water, energy and air, was nearing its end, which meant that BevSure was either going to renegotiate their terms or go with a competing supplier. This wasn't what made the vibe in the meeting room eerily tense, however—it was Sam Iddings, Purchasing Manager, who was making staff members feel uncomfortable. Within recent meetings and conversations with Aqua Co, they had (several times) not-so-subtly mentioned the possibility of raising their price for BevSure. This didn't worry Sam—he always succeeded at getting vendors to concede. He was primarily price and commodity focused; this—along with his surly attitude and stubbornness—certainly intimidated everybody (co-workers, vendors and customers). Sam didn't care, though. It was how he usually got others to comply with his demands.

His boss, however, the newly hired Marissa Morales, Director of Purchasing, was sick of it. She didn't like his attitude and thought his "never compromise" "strategy" to negotiating was outdated and professionally distasteful. At this particular meeting, she had informed all of the staff members of the Procurement department that they were to attend a two-day training workshop on Strategic Negotiation. Marissa believed that this would be beneficial to the entire department and that they would be able to immediately apply new negotiation strategies to their upcoming renegotiation of terms with Aqua Co. She was also hoping that it would change Sam's professional behavior and outlook towards negotiating. Marissa made it clear that attending this workshop was not a mere suggestion—it was mandatory for all Procurement department employees.

Most of the employees thought it was a good idea but Sam thought otherwise. Aside from being inherently stubborn in his ways, he was personally biased against anything that Marissa suggested as he thought he should have been promoted to Director of Purchasing. Sam was opposed to BevSure externally hiring somebody. Sam threw a verbal fit, which made his co-workers very uncomfortable.

–––

BevSure was a market leader in the brewing and beverage industry, and they had managed to keep it that way throughout the recession. It was nothing miraculous but it did seem that they were immune from the effects of the global economic environment's current vulnerability. Rather than experiencing a decrease in sales, the recession had actually spurned an increase in beverage sales as people still drank and purchased cheap soft drinks and alcoholic beverages. However, BevSure's business budgets were still tight, as it was in nearly every industry these days. The company cut costs wherever they could—they experienced a downsizing not too long ago and were even able to convince their agriculture supplier to reduce their water intake on the field, where many of their beverage ingredients were grown. Although no fermenting or distilling processes were conducted at BevSure, they did use a lot of filtered water to blend with concentrates, syrups and various infusions and flavors to create soft drinks. With more drinks to bottle came more water to filter, which meant that the facility not only needed more equipment to filter the water but more maintenance to manage its utilization.

Of course, Sam was interested in saving money and cutting corners wherever he could, which was why he was especially miffed at Aqua Co wanting to raise their price when the facility was working to significantly reduce their water intake and expenses. He knew that all other companies within the food and beverage industry were also in the same situation; this was probably the reason why Aqua Co was raising their price. Water was becoming scarcer, and more and more companies were becoming conscious about innovative water purification and maintenance, so Aqua Co saw this as an opportunity to raise its prices. It was a natural business move but that didn't mean that Sam would accept a higher price.

"There are other sustainable water solution companies that are doing the same thing as Aqua Co and I could just threaten the vendor with that," thought Sam to himself. "I can get them to concede, no problem."

Upset at the fact that he had to attend the training workshop, he made a mental note to himself that he would go with his initial "never compromise" plan when it came time to renegotiate terms with Aqua Co, regardless of whatever the workshop taught him and his co-workers. It was going to be a couple of weeks before Sam and the rest of the Procurement department were going to attend the workshop, anyway.

A Secret Meeting

Sam decided to jump the gun (behind Marissa's back, no less) by arranging a meeting with Aqua Co. He was sure that he could get them to concede and it would show his boss and co-workers that his technique was not outdated. In fact, he'd show them that it was still extremely effective. In his mind, he was going to kill two birds with one stone—he'd come out on top, looking like an office hero, and he would give Marissa a reason to not have all of Procurement attend the workshop.

Sam called up Patrick Howard, one of Aqua Co's key account managers and the primary point of contact for BevSure's Procurement department. Sam began the conversation by explaining how the company just could not afford to renew their contract with Aqua Co's increase in price. When Patrick tried to explain his side of the situation, Sam interjected.

"You know what, I can get this equipment and these services cheaper somewhere else."

"That may be true, but the cost of transition to another supplier may be more costly overall," Patrick replied. "Are you considering the total cost of ownership?"

Sam was taken aback by Patrick's reply, as he expected that the "I can get it cheaper somewhere else" remark usually began a new conversation in which the vendor would eventually concede. Sam and Patrick went back and forth with empty remarks, and the meeting ultimately went nowhere. It was clear that Patrick was set on not submitting to Sam's intimidation technique and the two managers agreed to continue the conversation at a more appropriate time during the renegotiation stage.

Sam thought about the situation after he hung up the phone, trying to come up with alternative solutions and options. He mulled over the idea of compromising but the problem with that was that it was just not his style. His stubbornness hindered him from thinking that compromising might benefit both BevSure and Aqua Co; he always relied on his "never compromise/make them concede" tactic and it had gotten him by for years now. Sam hated to even think it, but perhaps Marissa was making a good move by having him and his co-workers attend the workshop on Strategic Negotiation. He let out a sigh of disappointment and defeat at this thought.

Consequences of No Agreement (CNAs)

"Sam, can you come into my office, please?"

Sam tensed at the sound of Marissa saying his name. He grumbled, got up out of his seat and dragged his feet toward her office. He already knew what this was about and he didn't even try to show any sign of remorse. After taking a seat before Marissa's desk, Marissa began to talk about the hypothetical costs of choosing another vendor.

"There are a lot of other water services and maintenance organizations that are doing very innovative things with industries that have large water requirements. We can benefit from these services, like water recovery, re-use, automation for cooling water systems…very interesting and environmental things that would help us," Marissa stated.

"But if we can just get Aqua Co to concede to our price demands and explain how we absolutely cannot, and will not, comply with their higher price, we won't have to transition to another vendor. Just let me deal with Aqua Co, I've dealt with them before. I've dealt with a lot of other vendors before and I know what to do," Sam interjected.

"We are just talking about the possibility of moving to another vendor—a hypothetical situation in the case that Aqua Co does not concede. You've been in this position and in the business for long enough—you must understand that you must prepare for any kind of change and this may happen," Marissa remarked. Even though she hadn't been at BevSure for very long, it was obvious to her that Sam didn't like her and clearly thought that he should have been promoted to Director. He challenged her in every conversation. She had become all too familiar with Sam's stubbornness and was careful not to bring any more fuel to the

72

fire by getting frustrated or angry.

Marissa continued to talk. "Why don't you humor me for a little while and just treat this as a hypothetical situation. Here, let's try something new. I learned this from a book on strategic negotiations[9] [Sam scoffed] and I'm sure it's what you and your co-workers will be learning at the workshop in a few weeks. We'll start out by assessing the situation and come up with a list of consequences for both sides—the buyer and the vendor—if they do not agree. This list is called the CNAs (Consequences of No Agreement)."

"That's easy, if we don't agree on Aqua Co's price, then they lose the sale, and we'll take our business elsewhere," said Sam.

"Well, it's more than that. We should list all of the possible consequences and their value, monetary or otherwise, so we get a better idea of where each side stands in the situation," Marissa responded.

"Alright, alright," said Sam. (*Let's just get this over with*, he thought to himself.)

They brainstormed and came up with the following list of CNAs for both sides:

Buyer's side:
- Transition to another supplier = $1–$1.5 million
- Potential cost savings if Sam negotiates = 15–20 percent
- Management cost to change out 150 sites = $300K
- Loss of global partner who had delivered past net savings of $10+ million
- Alienating internal supporters/stakeholders (engineers, etc. who like Aqua Co)
- Risk to production (there is risk in changing vendors and possibly down time in manufacturing during transition)

---

[9] Brian J. Dietmeyer with Rob Kaplan, *Strategic Negotiation*.

Vendor's side:
- Loss of $7 million in short-term revenue
- Competitor would be empowered
- Loss of key reference
- Loss of sole supplier status (Aqua Co was the incumbent and only supplier)
- Loss of access to new markets and applications through BevSure R&D
- Combined total of approximately $15 million revenue at risk

Marissa and Sam stepped back and took a list at their list. Although they weren't sure of all the costs of each item, it was clear that the pain of changing suppliers would be significantly more than if they chose to stay with Aqua Co. Aqua Co was in the more empowered position because it seemed they had more to lose, but Marissa and Sam decided to ignore the unbalanced power.

Marissa ended their impromptu meeting with this and hoped that Sam would be cooperative with other beneficial ideas offered during the Strategic Negotiation workshop.

The Think! Inc. Workshop and Four-Step Negotiation Process

Sam and the rest of the Procurement department attended the workshop on Strategic Negotiation a few weeks later. The workshop was highly interactive and BevSure attendees were able to use real-life deals as examples in using the negotiation blueprinting process. The process was comprised of the following four steps:

1. Estimate the blueprint
   a. CNA Estimation: list the Consequences of No Agreement (CNAs) for both the buyer and vendor side
   b. Wish List Estimation: develop a list of items that the buyer and the vendor would ideally like to have in the deal; determine what is least and most important to each side

2. Validate the estimation

   a. Fact-check: validate the vendor's CNA and items on their Wish List by gathering information from:

      i. Your own knowledge of the vendor and your competitors

      ii. Knowledge of others in your organization who have either worked for the vendor or a competitor

      iii. Publicly available data (on-line searches, newspaper articles, annual reports, etc.)

      iv. The vendor themselves

3. Create value: create a list of items of value for both sides—use these items to trade with your vendor (this achieves a better solution dividing the joint value created)

4. Divide value: use the list of valuable items from Step 3 to create Multiple Equal Offers (MEOs) to the vendor—these offers are all equally acceptable to you, but are of varying value to the vendor

Sam's co-workers were impressed by how negotiating a deal was a strategic process—a clear-cut, analytical and measurable process. Sam's co-workers may have been wowed, but the whole workshop was in-one-ear-and-out-the-other for Sam. He was glad that they were provided a handout on the process, because he wasn't going to bother with taking any notes.

Throughout the workshop, Marissa would occasionally check up on Sam from her seat at the back of the room and noticed his lack of participation, note-taking and general nonchalance about the subject. When they returned from the workshop, she called Sam into her office.

She decided to be frank and said, "I noticed that you're still not convinced about working with the new negotiation process. It's clear that you're experiencing some difficulty with new methods of getting things done. I know that this is highly uncomfortable for you since you have been working as BevSure's Purchasing Manager for many years now but I want you to take a back seat for this renegotiation deal with Aqua Co. This is a big deal for us and I don't believe getting them to concede is the right approach. We have to compromise and going along with the new method of developing some trades and MEOs in order to create a better solution for all of us, is the best way to go. I will personally drive this deal. Please observe how I do it. You must start believing that there are other ways to do things."

Sam's anger boiled up inside of him at these words. As much as he wanted to fight, Marissa was his boss and throwing a verbal fit would only make things worse. He grumbled something that Marissa couldn't hear, got up out of his seat, and walked out of her office in a childish huff.

Marissa took that as Sam's concession.

Identifying Anchors

Wow, glad that is over with, thought Marissa after Sam left her office. She didn't want Sam's attitude to get her down so she quickly started working on outlining the Aqua Co deal with the new Strategic Negotiation process. She knew that Sam initially wanted BevSure to negotiate a lower price by at least 15 percent but, thinking that that was unreasonable, she began with softer targets. Since Aqua Co was letting them know of a price increase instead of a decrease, she was hoping that she could somehow get them to agree to a five to 10 percent price reduction (if they would agree to any kind of reduction at all). Marissa knew that she wasn't going to get this price reduction right off the bat and without giving anything in return so she had to also identify things of value to trade with Aqua Co.

Creating and Dividing Value

To move Aqua Co away from focusing on her requested price reduction, Marissa knew that creating value and listing potential trades for each side was her best bet in compromising and achieving more value. She outlined each side's potential trades:

Bevsure's potential trades:
- Longer contract (four to five years)
- Referrals to other food and beverage companies that could use Aqua Co's services

- Expand partnership globally—introduce them to five new global divisions
- Introduction to BevSure's other brands (although not in food service, there might be other opportunities for Aqua Co)

Aqua Co's potential trades:
- One to two year additional warranty service contract
- 24-hour response hotline for problems and issues
- Training on new water management process (re-using and recycling water)
- Diagnostic audit process to determine other ways BevSure can save
- Participation on Aqua Co's User Advisory Board to drive innovative new products and services (Marissa knew the Engineering Manager would want to do this)

Identifying Multiple Equal Offers (MEOs)

Based on the potential trades, Marissa jotted down some MEOs that she thought would be of interest to Aqua Co. This was the first time she had done anything like this and she was a little unsure of herself. But she believed in the new process so she was enthusiastic to give it a try.

After a few different drafts and outlines, she had three solid MEOs that she was pretty happy with.

Solid MEOs

Drive Down Cost	Innovation and Technology	Water and Energy Optimization
1 year contract	3 year contract	5 year contract
	5% disount	10% discount
Fee-based maintenance	1 year extension to warranty	2 years extension to warranty
Fee-based training	Fee-based training	Training for 20 employees

Solid MEOs (continued)

Drive Down Cost	Innovation and Technology	Water and Energy Optimization
	24-hour hotline access	24-hour hotline access
	Division referrals	Global referrals
		Free diagnostic and audit
		Participation on Advisory Board
		Access to BevSure R&D

Negotiation Results

Marissa was nervous the morning of her meeting with Aqua Co. She had an extra cup of coffee (which turned out to be a bad idea because it made her even more jittery and nervous) and practiced her MEO spiel in front of the bathroom mirror. She had it down, there was no doubt about that, but she felt like she needed some extra support. Once she was in the office, she found one of her best performing buyers, Katie Thompson, and recruited her to come along on the meeting; Marissa convinced herself that she was bringing her along for training purposes but really, she just didn't want to go alone.

They quickly walked past Sam's office. Marissa made a sudden stop, however, sighed, and took some hesitant steps back toward his office. She rapped on the door frame and said, "Why don't you come with me and Katie today to the meeting with Aqua Co? I know you're upset that you're not driving this deal but as the Purchasing Manager, I want you to see this new negotiation process in action. What do you say?"

After some reluctance, Sam agreed.

"You have to let me do the talking, though. I'm driving this deal as I have it all laid out," Marissa added.

"Fine by me," said Sam. (*I want to see your plan fall flat!* he thought.)

— — —

Marissa, Sam and Katie had their meeting with Patrick and his manager, John Joans, over lunch. Patrick kicked off the discussion bringing up Aqua Co's price with BevSure. Marissa pulled out her MEOs and went through each of the options with Patrick.

Patrick and John were clearly intrigued and impressed. They saw the third option as the best one as Aqua Co would get a longer contract with BevSure *and* much more opportunity than the other two options. The trades worked well for both sides. Providing training for 20 BevSure employees, access to their 24-hour hotline (which already existed within their company) and a free diagnostic audit wouldn't cost too much for Aqua Co, especially considering the longer contract and increased price they were getting from BevSure. Patrick also loved the idea of having a spot on BevSure's User Advisory Board—they would get to work *with* their client on new products and services instead of just working *for* them. This was good for both sides as it strengthened their customer-vendor relationship.

There was no question about it for Patrick. He was excited and wanted to move forward with their new contract. Marissa was over the moon; the process made the meeting go so smoothly and she felt great about the company's strengthened relationship with Aqua Co. She looked over at Sam after Patrick and John left their lunch meeting and although he was sitting at the table with his arms crossed, she could tell that he was shocked and impressed under his expressionless stare, but his body language told her he wasn't ready to admit it.

Epilogue

Once the contract was detailed and approved by the Legal department, BevSure and Aqua Co began working with their new agreement. The training worked splendidly and it made everyone in the company feel more confident and secure with the new water management process and equipment. Everybody loved having one of their vendors with creative ideas on the User Advisory Board and Marissa planned to propose this with her other vendors as it benefited both sides.

After seeing the Think! process work with a real-life deal, Sam warmed up just a little to the process. He didn't want to use it all the time (his stubbornness still got the best of him) but he sheepishly admitted to himself that Marissa's meeting with Aqua Co was more productive than one of his hot-headed meetings with vendors.

Lessons Learned

Sam learned a lot from this particular deal—he learned a lot about himself and about a new negotiation process that worked (only if you're willing to work with it, of course). His stubbornness and surly attitude got the best of him in this situation and it ultimately cost him his opportunity to renegotiate with Aqua Co but the only way he was going to believe in the Think! method was if he saw it in action to successfully bring in desired results. Marissa, on the other hand, was still unsure about Sam and intended to coach him a little while longer before making any decisions on his future employment at BevSure. He just didn't fit in with her strategic direction.

This deal brought to light that knowing your CNAs is key to adding value in a negotiation. CNAs set the boundaries for the Agreement Zone in any negotiation. Understanding the cost of the consequences will let buyers and sellers know which side is more empowered.

Case Study #3 – Falcon Theaters

"3-way Solution"

Situation Overview and Business Problem

Falcon Theaters prided itself on blockbuster movie showings and friendly customer service. Although they were not one of the largest North American theater chains, loyal customers returned to them because they always showed the latest releases and their staff was always helpful and service-minded. New customers chose them because they were relatively inexpensive compared to the larger theaters, charging $2–$3 less per ticket. Over the years, Falcon's quality customer service had resulted in extreme customer loyalty and it gradually became their trademark. Their staff members adhered to the "Service With a Smile" adage; this attitude gave Falcon a great reputation as customers lauded their friendliness and frequent visitors became loyal backers.

Naturally, the theaters put a lot of effort into advertising and relied on this to lure in new customers. But advertising was becoming more and more expensive and the competition was growing fierce.

Susan Goodman, Falcon's newly arrived Director and "rising star" of Operations and Provisioning, had been talking with Falcon managers about a steady increase in advertising costs. Management had been complaining about needed repairs and remodeling in the chain's 100 plus theaters. There was an urgent issue at hand—they needed to update their facilities and replace their video equipment immediately. Sometimes the projectors would fail and they would have to refund customers' admission price. This led to complaints and customer service problems—unacceptable to Falcon.

The increase in complaints when the systems didn't work and the decrease in customer satisfaction began imperceptibly. Susan had only been at Falcon as Director of Operations for a few months; in the midst of her new workload, the customer complaints overshadowed all other purchasing matters.

The New Director

Susan had begun her new position at the theater by applying her strong work ethic and sustaining Falcon's image. She was a recent MBA graduate from Arizona State University (ASU) and although she was young, she had had prior experience working at the headquarters of a major retailer. Before she had become Falcon's Director of Operations, she had worked in various departments, including Sales, Marketing and Purchasing. It was her experience coupled with her recent MBA that landed her the job as Director of Operations. (It did help, however, that Falcon Theaters was a smaller theater chain—she most likely would have a smaller role in larger, megaplex theater organizations.)

Since she was a recent graduate, she was knowledgeable about current business, corporation structures, techniques, etc. She had been interested and involved in business for practically her entire life—both of her parents were business professors and she had been interning or working at different kinds of companies and organizations since she was in college. In order to get her finances in order and to gain more experience, she began working full-time after undergrad and before she began her MBA program at ASU. Being a big-picture thinker and having a habit of planning ahead, Susan pursued Falcon's job opening with sheer determination. After a long interview process and many weeks of constantly refreshing her e-mail inbox, she finally received an offer from Falcon. She began as a Digital Marketer and gradually climbed the ladder to Director of Operations within a couple of years.

Susan spent a couple of months at this new position getting the lay of the land and settling in. She began to understand more about the cost structure of the company, and decided to help by cutting costs wherever she could. She knew that Falcon was competing against larger, and more competitive, megaplex theaters, and she wanted to spend more time, effort and money in keeping Falcon's image efficient, reliable and friendly. Falcon had already laid off redundant employees and reduced the cost with the theater's beverage vendor. Susan even took on a few extra responsibilities. She also raised movie tickets (just slightly) to bring in more revenue. Even with this price increase, Falcon was still relatively inexpensive compared to their competition.

Although her strong work ethic and swift decision making on cutting costs and laying off employees made her seem like she had a tough exterior, she was very approachable, reasonable and a joy to work with as a

Director—nothing less than what Falcon employees and customers were used to in a staff member, even if she was upper management.

On the Fritz Again
Investigating and Validating the Problem

When Susan attended her first staff meeting as Director six months ago, one of the inspectors mentioned that there were 104 faulty or broken projectors in their 108 theaters. That was approximately one broken or faulty projector per theater. Each theater had four to six screens and spare projectors so at the time, one faulty projector per theater did not seem like such a large amount. As this issue was mentioned in passing and on her first day, Susan only made a mental note and put this concern on the back burner. She wanted to direct her focus and attention on trimming her staff down to their most reliable and efficient employees and creating a bond between her staff and her boss, Dave Langer, the Vice President and General Manager, who was coaching her. By the time her six-month mark came around, she had created some solid, professional relationships with her staff, as well as gained the trust of Dave.

Dave had lauded Susan's impressive work at Falcon many times throughout her past six months as Director. But he then began to notice the increase of faulty projectors as well as several customer complaints about them. He mentioned this to Susan, firmly stating that he had faith in her ability to come up with a creative solution that didn't cost the company an exorbitant amount of money.

Susan surely did not want to let Dave down and although she was confident in her work, she was undoubtedly wary about coming up with a solution that would fix this problem, considering that the theaters were under such a tight budget already. She began by taking a look at the number of faulty projectors that had been mounting and let out a hefty sigh when she saw it: 198 (approximately two projectors per theater). How this number had doubled within the last six months was surprising, but their old age (they were at least ten years old) was apparently the cause.

To see the problem first-hand, Susan went into one of Falcon's theaters that had three faulty projectors. She went to each of them and fiddled around with the buttons and viewing options. One of the projectors would not turn on and the other two just did not work properly (e.g., the quality of the movie shown was poor and snowy and/or would take a long while to turn on).

Susan regretted putting this issue in the back of her mind six months ago because now the projectors' demise was imminent; even if the theater could come up with the funds to replace the faulty projectors, the other currently-working projectors would soon fail to work and require replacements as well. She knew that the ultimate result, at the bare minimum, would be to replace the projectors with new upgraded ones since the ones that the theaters currently had were out-of-date, of poor quality and were obsolete models anyway. She was looking at a cost of nearly $3–$5 million.

Although Susan knew that Falcon's already small budget did not allow much wiggle room for this kind of expense, she decided to give the manufacturer a call to see if there was any hope of an affordable replacement price or perhaps, just perhaps, a possible discount. Susan spoke to the manufacturer's Sales department and explained Falcon's situation, emphasizing that the theater was on a tight budget. Sales told her that it would cost approximately $5 million for Falcon to replace their projectors with upgraded ones.

The phone call ended with Susan thinking one thing: there was absolutely no way Falcon could afford to replace the projectors within this year's budget. There had to be some other source of funding that she could come up with to fix the problem.

The Think! Inc. Workshop and Four-Step Negotiation Process

In preparation for her new position at Falcon, and knowing that business negotiation was inevitably going to be a part of any job she was looking for, Susan attended a two-day Strategic Negotiation workshop. This was more than six months ago, however, and although she had applied some of the knowledge and practices that she had learned to a re-negotiation of a vendor contract at Falcon, she could not fully recall the negotiation process off the top of her head. She referred back to her notes and a copy of *Strategic Negotiation* to refresh her memory.

What she was particularly interested in was how the negotiation process emphasized the concept that negotiation was an analytical business process rather than a haphazard, immeasurable idea, primarily driven by a series of behaviors.[10] Being an analytical and strategic thinker, this way of thinking appealed to her.

She began by looking at the four-step process that she had outlined in her notes:

1. Estimate the blueprint

    a. CNA Estimation: list the Consequences of No Agreement (CNAs) for both the buyer and vendor side

    b. Wish List Estimation: develop a list of items that the buyer and the vendor would ideally like to have in the deal; determine what is least and most important to each side

2. Validate the estimation

    a. Fact-check: validate the vendor's CNA and items on their Wish List by gathering information from:

        i. Your own knowledge of the vendor and your competitors

        ii. Knowledge of others in your organization who have either worked for the vendor or a competitor

        iii. Publicly available data (newspaper articles, annual reports, etc.)

        iv. The vendor themselves

3. Create value: create items of value for both sides—you will use these items to trade with your vendor (this achieves a better solution)

4. Divide value: use your list of valuable items from Step 3 to create

---

[10] Brian J. Dietmeyer with Rob Kaplan, *Strategic Negotiation*, 3.

MEOs to the vendor—these offers are all equally acceptable to you but are of varying value to the vendor

As Susan reviewed her notes, it was clear that Falcon's situation was tough. She was in a quandary about trades for her side. What could she possibly offer as a trade? And, even with the discount, Falcon would not be able to afford the projectors on their current budget. She could arrange a meeting with the manufacturer, a vendor for over 10 years, but she could not figure out a way to create a better situation for the both of them. Essentially, what Susan wanted was an affordable replacement price and she just did not believe that the manufacturer would be able to provide the level of discount she was looking for.

If there was anything she learned from the workshop, it was to never concede on price—always create and divide value to make things beneficial for both sides. She thought about this and after some deep thought, Susan came up with the idea of bringing more parties into the solution. This would make it easier to develop a larger list of valuable items (i.e., a larger Wish List) that they could all trade with each other.

The More the Merrier

After racking her brain over it, she finally came up with something that seemed so obvious that she wondered why she didn't think of it sooner: pre-screening advertisements! It seemed like one of those so-crazy-it-had-to-work ideas, but if she could approach a large television network, large shopping center or other businesses, and have them advertise their programs to Falcon customers before the showing of a movie, it would most likely generate enough funds to significantly help with the projectors' replacement cost. Showing advertisements before the movie feature was common in megaplex theaters so why wouldn't it work for Falcon?

She approached Dave and the Board of Directors with her idea and they agreed that it was a good creative solution that just might work. They encouraged her to go ahead and arrange a meeting with the local television network affiliate as a first contact and introduction to the national networks. Susan was proud of herself for coming up with this idea and she felt confident that she could get the network on board but, thinking back, she knew she had to outline her negotiation process before arranging a meeting with them.

Identifying Priorities

After introducing her idea to the Board of Directors, she and the board members brainstormed about what kind of advertisements would be most attractive to the network and to Falcon Theater customers. The new Fall television season was upon them, which meant that television audiences were looking forward to new series and season premieres. This was an important ratings season for television networks so Falcon was sure that giving the network another outlet to advertise on would be extremely attractive.

Deciding to go with that as her opening, Susan then had to think about the projector manufacturer. Going along with her advertising idea, her thought process naturally led her to come up with the idea of providing an advertising spot for them, too.

Identifying these priorities made her realize that trades are not limited to just Ts & Cs and price, something that had also been touched upon during the workshop. The analytical thinker in Susan truly believed in this and she was determined to come up with other non-price-related trades that might be offered.

Creating and Dividing Value

The next step after identifying trades was to validate the priorities. Trades would ultimately expand the pie so all parties would benefit from the deal. Susan made a list of what Falcon had to offer the network and then followed it up with a list of what she thought the network and manufacturer had to offer.

Falcon's potential trades:
- Advertising spots for the network's Fall television programs $3–$5 million/year

- Targeted demographics information for matching with network programs (probably worth $100K to the networks if they had to pay for it)
- Advertising for the manufacturer of their new line of home projectors $500K

Network's potential trades:

- Program shorts for targeted demographics $3–$5 million/yr
- Paid advertisements of Fall television programs for specific demographics $1 million/yr
- Connection to other companies that may be interested in advertising

Projector manufacturer's potential trades:

- Discounted replacement price 15–20 percent
- Latest model of projectors with warranty protection $100K per year
- Two-hour service level agreement
- Call center support 24/7

Establishing the Offer

After identifying value and creating lists of potential trades for all parties involved, Susan contacted the network affiliate with her idea. Susan called Gloria Tan, the local head of advertising, and introduced herself. Gloria referred Susan to network advertising chief, Ronald Ellis. After some small talk and pleasantries, she presented her idea to him and explained the opportunity to expand their advertising at Falcon Theaters. She explained that Falcon customers were of varied demographics and they would be able to advertise different types of programs that would appeal to many different audiences. Falcon had the data on people, income levels and preferences and she was prepared to trade it. She even mentioned the possibility of having her own staff members maintain these activities (e.g., getting the advertisements loaded onto the projectors, coordinating the distribution of DVDs for the entire chain, being the primary point of contact in updating the ads monthly, etc.).

There seemed to be no hesitation on Ron's side about the possibility of advertising at Falcon Theaters. The Fall season was an important time for television networks' ratings as they were coming back from a stagnant Summer season and wanted to entice audiences with their new and continuing programs. They believed this to be a great opportunity.

Susan was ecstatic at hearing their enthusiasm. They ended their phone call with a scheduling of a face-to-face meeting to discuss the offers and details. Susan next called the projector manufacturer to let them know what was going on. They too, were intrigued with the idea of paid advertisements for their own new products.

Soon thereafter, Susan met with the network's Advertising team to discuss the details of the deal.

Negotiation Results

After Susan's face-to-face meeting with the network, she had gotten much more than she had initially hoped for. When the problem of the faulty projectors had initially arose and eventually worsened, all she wanted was for the theater to find some way to replace them with upgraded models. After coming up with the idea of selling advertisements, she found that the solution benefitted all parties.

- Upgraded projectors at a 20 percent discounted price (savings of $1 million)
  - Advertising spots for projector manufacturer's products in exchange for discount
- 24/7 support
- Five-year warranty on projectors
- Advertising spots for network programs: new revenue paid $4.5 million/year in exchange for specific demographics theater by theater

Epilogue

With the money from advertisements, Falcon was able to afford the projectors' replacement costs and earn nearly $2 million in addition annual revenue. All of Falcon's theaters received brand new upgraded projectors. New and frequent customers were extremely happy with the better quality of the theaters' movie showings.

This deal was an incredible accomplishment for Susan as she proved that her young age and inexperience were not hindrances in getting a great deal if she just applied the Strategic Negotiation concepts.

Lessons Learned

During this particular deal, Susan had learned that creativity in problem-solving was a must. Coupled with a Strategic Negotiation process, there were better solutions to every problem and every deal. Creating and dividing value was the key driving force in achieving her goal as well as the foundation of Strategic Negotiation.

Case Study #4 – Oil and Pipe Fitting Inc. (OPF)
Part 1: Speedy Logistics

"Bankrupt!"

Situation Overview and Business Problem

BANKRUPT.

The word was first bandied about the office hallways of Oil and Pipe Fitting Inc. (OPF) a few years ago as employees gradually became aware of the company's rising debt. An initial act of desperation led the company to extend payment times for their vendors. After a while, however, OPF's vendors justifiably began demanding their overdue payments.

In the beginning, executive management was careful not to say anything about the possibility of going bankrupt but the hushed pieces of discreet conversations and impromptu meetings behind closed doors fed the rumor mill. Nosy employees would conveniently pass by, hoping to catch a word or two.

In spite of the booming oil industry, and after meticulously dissecting the situation during several meetings, the Board of Directors realized that the problem was ultimately mismanagement, both hierarchically and financially.

A few years ago, OPF's CEO, Marcus Boyce, began to prepare for his retirement as he had worked at the company for over 60 years. His successor (and only son), Stephen Boyce, became the new CEO. It was obvious that the only reason Stephen became the CEO was because of his father; he clearly did not have much business management experience. He had graduated from MBA school about five years earlier and had been working at OPF ever since. He was generally viewed as a slacker student, never paying much attention to his studies or caring about anything except himself. If one of his peers had the gall to condescendingly ask Stephen exactly what he was doing in grad school, he would just bring up the fact that his great-grandfather founded the pipe and fitting company over 100 years ago, as if it was a valid justification for his attendance. (Grandpa had also donated enough money to build the new Business building at the university.) Having gotten used to everything being handed to him, Stephen carried on this attitude into his work life; he was a playboy and didn't actually want to do any of the hard work of managing the company.

Since its founding, OPF had become a leading oil field parts and fittings manufacturer for the oil industry. The privately held company operated globally and had manufacturing and sales offices in the United States, Canada, Mexico, England, Brazil, China, Saudi Arabia and the United Arab Emirates.

As CEO, Stephen was ultimately placed in charge of 27,500 people worldwide despite the fact that he clearly did not have the business experience, or the desire to learn about the business. He wielded his title and used it as a power play over the OPF employees. He was even known to shamelessly use it as a pick-up line in bars and at parties. The company quickly learned to run its daily operations without his guidance, however, and left him to be the face of OPF, only keeping him in the loop about major decisions.

But things began to unravel quickly when OPF's largest customer, Solution Oil, an oil field developer, went out of business. As a direct result, Solution Oil was unable to pay their debts to their vendors, putting OPF in a precarious position. Solution Oil wasn't the only one. Due to mismanagement of OPF Accounting and Finance, there were many other late-paying customers, bad debt and severe cash flow problems.

The Board of Directors saw only one solution at this point: BANK-RUPTCY. Once all the executives had accepted the company's situation and realized what had to be done, it became clear that filing for Chapter 11 was the best solution. They viewed this as a temporary situation as it would give them time to reorganize their business, cut costs and come out of bankruptcy with leaner, more efficient operations. They filed for Chapter 11 Bankruptcy and began to drastically cut costs wherever they could—the first thing to go was Stephen. It was a no-brainer decision and legally, his employment contract terms were suspended under Chapter 11. In fact, in the grand scheme of things, the Board saw it as the easiest decision. The real problem was figuring out how they would reorganize and emerge out of bankruptcy.

— — —

It had been a few months now since Stephen was fired and since then, the company had brought in a well-known turn-around consultant,

Robert Waugh, as their new Chief Operating Officer.

Robert was in his mid-60s and had been a consultant for over 20 years. He had plenty of experience reorganizing companies and usually pulled companies out of bankruptcy by driving out costs in Purchasing, Manufacturing, and Distribution. One of the primary targets for driving out some of these costs at OPF was with their main supplier, Speedy Logistics, an outsourced logistics company that was responsible for running OPF's warehouse and delivery operations.

Investigating and Validating the Problem

Before calling Speedy to ask them questions about their operations, Robert knew it would be best to do some research on his own about their business relationship with OPF.

Speedy Logistics took care of all of OPF's distribution needs. The entirety of OPF's finished goods inventory was stored at Speedy in the U.S., which meant that every time customers placed an order for OPF products, Speedy would be the one to retrieve, pack and ship those orders. Since they were responsible for OPF's entire inventory (including U.S.-made products as well as products shipped in from China), OPF had granted them access to their IT systems. Although Speedy wasn't able to view forecasts on these systems, they relied on OPF systems daily to view orders that were scheduled for shipment and to help control inventory information.

Speedy's reliability in completing orders was on par most of the time—their reports indicated that they filled orders 98 percent accurately and 97 percent on time. They were only two to three percentage points away from perfection, and Speedy largely attributed this small gap to not being able to view OPF's forecasts. The company was vocal about it; they took every appropriate opportunity to bring up the fact that if only they were able to view the forecasts, they would be able to schedule enough people to work at peak times and improve the order fulfillment rates. But every time it was to no avail; OPF felt that sales and shipment forecasts were completely confidential corporate information and they were just not comfortable sharing these with Speedy.

Before Stephen had been fired, he had been the person managing the OPF-Speedy relationship, but it was more social than anything. There was no need for Stephen to talk business or money with Speedy as their contract automatically renewed every year and the two companies had not conducted a competitive bid for over 10 years. Speedy simply kept renewing the relationship by taking Stephen out to extravagant dinners and providing trips on their company yacht. Stephen loved doing this, often bringing a girlfriend along for the weekend cruises. Stephen would not allow Purchasing to get involved in this relationship and simply told the Purchasing Manager to renew the contract every year.

– – –

Robert Waugh mulled over the situation and wrote notes as he thought about it. He decided that it would be best to arrange a meeting with the CEO of Speedy to bolster and maintain their relationship (and to investigate a little). He wanted to keep the relationship close, provide a positive image and experience with OPF because frankly, Robert ultimately wanted a 15 to 20 percent price reduction from them. Looking at their contract, he felt that OPF was being overcharged by Speedy and, with the word BANKRUPTCY looming over OPF, the company couldn't afford to be overcharged for anything.

There was one big problem that was driving a wedge between the two companies, however: late payments. Since OPF filed for bankruptcy, they were unable to pay Speedy on time so Speedy, naturally, was not able to pay their own warehouse workers without borrowing against their line of credit at the bank. Robert knew it would be difficult to maintain a positive relationship with Speedy as they were already unhappy about OPF's late payments. But Robert knew that he had to try since he was sure that they could come to an agreement and possibly trade things of value with each other.

Robert was familiar with the Strategic Negotiation process from a previous company where a colleague had applied the principles. He was very intrigued and impressed with the concept and the positive outcome. It made sense to have an organized approach to the negotiation process and to think of it analytically rather than as a series of behaviors.[11] Robert was anxious to use this method to see if he could map out a plan, not only to maximize the cost reduction with Speedy, but to also create gains in value for both companies.

Consequences of No Agreement (CNAs)

The first thing Robert had to do was to think about what would happen if OPF and Speedy couldn't come to an agreement (the Conse quences of No Agreement). If the conversations with Speedy went badly, it was possible that Speedy would cease their business relationship with OPF entirely. This would leave OPF in the position of having to scramble to find a new provider very quickly. It would probably mean they would have to shut down shipping products, and thus billing for them, for a period until the new warehouse was up and running. There would also be a steep learning curve for any new warehouse provider. Further, new vendors would be skeptical regarding OPF's bankruptcy situation.

No, changing logistics vendors was not a good idea. Although moving on to other areas of the company to try to reduce costs and prices elsewhere was also on Robert's agenda, he was sure that he could reduce OPF's cost with Speedy by at least 20 percent.

He came up with a short list of each side's CNA:

OPF's side (Buyer):

- Risk of not being able to contract with new vendor due to bankruptcy—total catastrophe: unable to ship
- Damaged relationship with Speedy
- Potential for disruption in shipping (could cost up to $1 million)
- Painful transition to another logistics company—a lot of work for many OPF people ($500K)
- Long learning curve for new vendor

---

[11] Brian J. Dietmeyer with Rob Kaplan, *Strategic Negotiation*.

Speedy's side (Vendor):

- Loss of $22 million in annual revenue
- Loss of major customer
- Loss of reputation in the Oil & Gas industry
- Lay-offs of warehouse workers and supervisory staff

Clearly, OPF had the biggest economic risk, but both sides had extremely high risk. OPF could possibly lose their entire business if the two companies couldn't come to terms. Having to shut down shipping while they changed to a new logistics provider could be disastrous. It would also be a catastrophic loss for Speedy. Roger recognized that Speedy had more power in this negotiation, but he still intended to do his best negotiating.

After taking a look at his list, Robert knew that when it came time to talk to the Speedy CEO about renegotiating their contract, he would have to be honest, appeal to their long-term relationship and demonstrate that this was good for both sides.

Well, perhaps I can come up with some good trades for them, Robert thought. He also thought that the company needed to make their relationship with Speedy more professional and start hosting meaningful Quarterly Business Reviews to keep the relationship objectives and on-track.

Robert moved on to the next step of the process: creating and dividing value.

Creating and Dividing Value

Robert knew that coming up with trades was the next important step. If possible, he wanted to keep both companies happy and create benefits for everybody while still saving money for OPF. He needed to look for things that were of uneven value to each side so they could be traded.

The first obvious trade that OPF could give Speedy was a longer contract (although this might not look so appealing to Speedy since OPF was currently behind in payments). The second one was to finally provide

100

Speedy access to the OPF forecasts they had been asking for years. This would improve Speedy's planning, performance and operations and get Speedy's accuracy and timeliness percentage up, while allowing them to plan work hours more effectively. Robert thought this access would be a good trade for at least a 10 percent discount on Speedy's services. After all, with better efficiency, Speedy would be saving costs.

After racking his brain for more potential trades that OPF could do with Speedy, he couldn't come up with anything. But two trades didn't seem like enough. So Robert decided to do some more research on Speedy to see if he could find out any information that would lead to more trades. After some investigation via online searches and quickly perusing everything he could about Speedy Logistics, he found out that they had facilities in the Netherlands, Dubai UAE and Shenzhen, China. It was as if a CFL light bulb went on!

OPF could offer to invest some money for Speedy to convert these facilities into distribution centers for OPF goods, provided that the bankruptcy judge would allow it. OPF would be expanding their global services, gaining more customers around the world at better response times and Speedy would be receiving support directly from OPF to build them. Operations could start up quickly. Robert was happy about finding this information and he was sure that Speedy would be happy about his investment offer.

He then outlined each company's list of potential trades.

OPF's potential trades:
- Longer contract (one to five years)
- Access to forecasts (10–15 percent efficiency gain for Speedy)
- Investment in building out distribution centers internationally $2 million

Speedy's potential trades:
- Price reduction five to 10 percent
- Improved fill rate from 98 to 99 percent
- Quarterly Business Reviews

Identifying Multiple Equal Offers (MEOs)

After outlining OPF's and Speedy's potential trades, developing the MEOs to present to Speedy came easy. Robert used his list of trades and research, then went right into creating three Multiple Equal Offers. Below is a chart of his offers, each aptly named to reflect their primary focus:

Robert's MEO Offers

One More Year	Foresight	Global Supply Chain
1 year contract	3 year contract	5 year contract
Cost Reduction 10%	Cost Reduction 20%	Cost Reduction 25%, graduated 10% in year 1; 20% in year 2 and 25% in years 3–5
Quarterly Business Reviews with newly established KPIs and a focus on cost reduction every quarter	Quarterly Business Reviews with newly established KPIs and a focus on cost reduction every quarter	Quarterly Business Reviews with newly established KPIs and a focus on cost reduction every quarter
Improve fill rate to sustainable 99% accuracy and 98% on time	Improve fill rate to sustainable 99% accuracy and 98% on time	Improve fill rate to sustainable 99.5% accuracy and 99% on time
	Share systems forecast on a monthly basis so Speedy can improve their operations planning	Allow Speedy access to OPF systems for daily view of forecasts
		Develop partnership plan to fully integrate operations, including Executive leadership meetings
		OPF to invest $2 million immediately for Speedy to build out distribution centers in Netherlands and China (pending approval by bankruptcy judge)
		Speedy and OPF negotiate with transportation companies for additional 10% cost reduction and share reduction 50/50

Robert stepped back and took a look at his chart. He was feeling good about what he came up with and hoped that Speedy would be impressed with these options. In addition to the list of trades he had developed earlier, he came up with one more thing to make the deal more enticing. He would bring up the idea of reducing transportation costs by working with Speedy to negotiate with transportation companies. The benefits here would mostly accrue to OPF, but Speedy could also use these new rates for their other customers.

Negotiation Results

Robert called the CEO of Speedy, Ellen Schmidt, to schedule a meeting with her. When he told her that it was a meeting to renegotiate their contract, she heaved a big sigh and gave a begrudged reply. It was clear that she was already not happy about OPF's bankruptcy, their late payments and disintegrating business relationship after Stephen's departure. She wasn't surprised that he had called. It didn't faze Robert, though, as he expected as much after the Chapter 11 Bankruptcy filing. Nothing less than a desire to cut costs and reduce prices from their service suppliers was normal. Also, he was pretty sure that Ellen would be more than satisfied with any of the MEOs he was going to present to her.

They met over a business lunch and eased into the renegotiation conversation. Robert pulled out his MEO chart and went over each with Ellen. With each MEO, Robert could see Ellen's attitude changing. She was irritated at the beginning of lunch as she clearly didn't want to reduce their pricing with OPF. She sat hunched over, annoyed and disconnected from the conversation but gradually sat up straighter and began to smile as Robert explained the benefits of each of the offers.

Each offer sounded better than the last. Ellen was especially interested in the third option, "Global Supply Chain." Although this option meant giving OPF a 25 percent cost reduction, it would happen over a period of five years. They would begin with just a 10 percent reduction the first year and then it would graduate by 10 percent the second year, and then up to 25 percent over the last few years. Ellen thought this was completely reasonable as Speedy was also gaining other benefits from OPF's trades. They would finally be given daily access to OPF's forecasts, thus being able to optimize their operations. This, in turn, would bump up their fill rate because they would be able to schedule enough warehouse workers during peak times and reduce last-minute overtime. Ellen was particularly excited about Robert's offer to invest money in using Speedy's international distribution centers for OPF goods and the opportunity to work with OPF on improving their partnership by having executive leadership meetings and Quarterly Business Reviews.

Robert is a pretty good guy, thought Ellen.

It was clear that both companies benefited the most from the last option and Ellen was happy to continue serving OPF; after all, they had been Speedy's largest customer for 10 years.

Epilogue

OPF and Speedy decided on the five-year contract and "Global Supply Chain" approach. The bankruptcy judge approved the investment because the business case that Robert presented was substantial. After the new contract was signed, everything seemed to fall into place. It was like a domino effect. Although Robert had initially wanted a 20 percent reduction that was effective immediately, OPF benefited even more in the long-term. The company began by saving 10 percent in their original pricing with Speedy but the new terms improved Speedy's operations performance substantially. They were able to plan their work hours according to the forecasts on OPF's IT systems, and were extremely productive and accurate with OPF orders. This, coupled with the news that OPF was gradually pulling out of bankruptcy, influenced new customers to purchase from OPF and made old customers trust the company again. This also increased Speedy's business as they were known in the logistics community for assisting in the turn-around.

Lessons Learned

Robert ended up developing a superbly beneficial and better solution for both companies using the Think! Inc. Strategic Negotiation methodology. Robert learned that creating solutions that were good for both sides—the buyer and the vendor—was the best solution for bringing a company out of debt and bankruptcy. Bankrupt companies are usually focused solely on reducing their pricing with vendors, cutting costs wherever they can, borrowing more money, etc. but it is crucial to keep in mind that maintaining positive relationships with existing vendors and/or customers is just as important. Creating value for both sides in their negotiations was a win for all parties.

Case Study #5 – OPF Part 2: Braemar Oilfield Contractors

"Customers Affect Procurement"

Introduction

Robert Waugh sat up in his bed after another restless night. For the last few months, his sleep had been continually interrupted with dreams of work or a string of over-analytical and panicked thoughts. He had recently become acting COO at Oil and Pipe Fitting Inc. (OPF) after successfully negotiating a longer contract and 25 percent cost reduction with their outsourced logistics company, Speedy Logistics. The OPF board and executives were quite pleased with his work to date. Robert was initially brought on as a consultant to help pull OPF out of bankruptcy and although the company was still in trouble, he had alleviated much of their financial pain with the Speedy negotiation. He had consulted for countless companies throughout his career and had helped many of them recover from bankruptcy but still, it was no easy job. As rewarding as it was to help companies gain back their confidence and financial standing, Robert felt helpless at times at OPF.

Although the oil industry was relatively recession-proof, suppliers like OPF were still struggling with price pressure from both customers and vendors. The demand for oil never seemed to let up, and neither did the relentless price reduction demands from customers. The oil industry was full of demanding and difficult "oil men."

This forced Robert up at 6:30 a.m. every morning. Not only did the OPF employees need the company to stay in business, customers were depending on them, too. As he got ready for work, Robert thought about the deal that he had helped OPF with when he first arrived at the company. He was proud of how he handled the Speedy Logistics situation and he—along with the rest of the company—was pleased with the results. Both OPF and Speedy benefited from the situation; OPF got the longer contract and intended cost reduction they wanted and Speedy got more access to OPF's IT systems, access to the executive leadership and Quarterly Business Reviews. In addition to that, OPF began investing in the building of Speedy distribution centers in the Netherlands and China, which was advantageous for both parties.

Global development with Speedy was a very creative breakthrough. Coming up with things to offer vendors when the company was going bankrupt had been difficult, to say the least. But thinking about how smoothly that negotiation process went, and how effectively the Think! Inc. methodology worked, made him smile. It gave him confidence that the company could eventually get themselves out of bankruptcy if they bolstered their business relationships (whether they were with customers or vendors) by adding value for everyone. Robert had learned that practically every business problem involving two parties could work out positively if people worked at creating and dividing value.

He tried to keep this in mind when he turned his thoughts over to Braemar Oilfield Contractors. Braemar was an oil exploration and production company and had been in business since the early 20th century in Taft, California when the oil business was a young but flourishing industry. Pipe fitting companies had been in Taft to supply parts to oil companies from the very beginning.

Taft was a town located about 30 miles outside of Bakersfield, CA and was one of the few remaining towns in the U.S. that existed solely because of nearby oil reserves. It sat in a major petroleum and gas production region, directly on the Midway-Sunset oil field, where many leading oil companies, including Braemar, conducted their operations. The town revolved around oil and it prided itself on its profits made from the oil and gas industry. Huge oil production machinery—like steam injection wells, steam generators and producing wells that find and pump oil and water up out of the ground—were situated along the flat desert area. Robert had made a visit to Taft recently and it was quite a scene to behold. Massive machinery was perpetually pumping against beautiful looming mountains in the background. The town's pride in being a part of the oil industry was evident in their rough and tumble cowboy approach to life and their "Oil Dorado" festival days. It was obvious that oil and gas production was still booming, due to the world's insatiable thirst for oil.

Robert met many Braemar employees on his visit. The ones working in the field were an interesting, rough-rider lot—*machismo* men who worked outside with rigs, drills and pumps all day. Robert asked several of them what the most important thing to them was, out there working firsthand with the machinery. Several different employees responded that it was having the materials and supplies they needed available immediately when they needed them. Despite being around for over a century, the industry was still developing quickly and it was important to keep up with the latest production techniques and equipment. It hindered production when they had to wait for materials or parts to arrive when something broke or when Braemar was in the process of developing new fields.

Robert learned that although oil production was always in high demand, it had peaked and declined several times within the last century. Technological advances, however, had helped the industry find more oil, which was why Braemar was interested in purchasing more materials and supplies from OPF. They were looking to develop several new drilling fields in and/or around Taft. OPF had worked closely with Braemar to develop several new pieces of equipment that returned about $500,000 in royalty payments to OPF each year.

OPF had been selling materials and supplies to Braemar—everything from tanks to fittings, pipes to flanges—for 30 years. But despite their loyalty and long business relationship, and instead of being sympathetic towards OPF's bankruptcy situation, Braemar seemed to be taking advantage of OPF's precarious financial state and recently asked for a further discount.

"Cowboys," thought Robert. (Apparently the new Braemar CFO, Raymond Berg, was on a mission to drive down parts costs.)

Robert sighed, and finished getting ready for work.

Situation Overview and Business Problem

Braemar's request for a cost reduction wasn't completely unprecedented. They had informed OPF of their plans to develop several new drilling fields and since Braemar bought 75 percent materials and supplies from OPF, a big transaction between the two companies was to be expected—perhaps even a blanket purchase order for a year or more. This would be a very big deal for OPF. But after OPF informed them of their Chapter 11 filing, Braemar came back to the company with their cost reduction demand. Robert knew that OPF was in no position to turn down Braemar as a customer; that would only worsen OPF's situation.

Of course, Braemar knew this and saw this as an opportunity to reduce their own costs.

Ray Berg is probably laughing to himself, thought Robert. *The jerk.*

Robert was frustrated that Ray was making this so hard for OPF to begin their own financial recovery. Given the circumstances, however, it was not completely unexpected.

When Robert arrived at OPF that morning, he walked into the Purchasing department to see how things were going. OPF produced their products at their nearby factory. They bought raw materials and components for the factory to use on the production line. Robert knew that if Braemar was going to pinch OPF on the sales price, then OPF would also need price reductions from its own raw materials vendors.

Liz Hsu, OPF's Purchasing Manager, was on the telephone with a new vendor.

"How's it going, Liz?" asked Robert after Liz hung up the phone.

"Okay. I was speaking to a new supplier just now about purchasing the raw materials we need to build for Braemar but we didn't make much progress since I'm not sure where we stand on this project. What's going on? I just told our supplier to hold off a bit until we know how the new project is going to pan out with Braemar and the volume of materials we will need for the build. The vendor is anxious to get a purchase order from us."

"Liz, we need to slow down," Robert said calmly. "We are still working on the Braemar deal. It's complicated *(especially since Ray has been phoning me every day about it)* but I'm sure we will come up with a solution that benefits both parties. I'm not ready to give in to a price reduction with Braemar without trying to gain some things for us, too. Once we have a Braemar deal, you'll need to go to work on your vendors to get their prices down."

"Okay, okay, you know I'm just worried," Liz replied. "What you did with the Speedy Logistics deal was so impressive. You mentioned that you had used some sort of negotiation technique to come up with optimal solutions. Do you think you can apply the same technique with the Braemar situation? You know, so we could perhaps negotiate a better deal? Maybe you could even teach me about the new approach."

"Yes, I'm going to try at least. The thing that is unique for me about this situation is that Braemar is a customer. I've pretty much just worked with vendors on turn-arounds but I'm going to try and leverage the same concepts for this negotiation with our customer. I don't think the process will be too different."

"Okay, well, that makes me feel a bit better," Liz said.

"Ha, well, thanks, Liz. I'll keep you posted," Robert replied as he exited her office.

Investigating and Validating the Problem

Robert set up a meeting with Ray at Braemar to talk to him about their situation. He was hoping that this meeting would reveal some information about Braemar that he could use to develop Braemar's CNA and discover some potential trades. Robert determined to keep the meeting friendly, no matter how much Ray bugged him.

"Ray, Braemar has been such a loyal customer of OPF for the last 30 years. You guys have renewed your contract time and again and we appreciate that. We're partners and we're friends and we're absolutely grateful that you've stuck with us during this precarious financial situation of ours. I want to continue to make you guys happy with us. Can you tell me what is the most important thing to Braemar right now and how can we help with that?"

"Cost! Cost! Cost! Cost! Of course, it's the cost, Robert," Ray declared obnoxiously. "We're competing against other major oil and gas development companies and with new technological advances on oil machinery and production, we need to develop more drilling fields. We need to do it fast, too, because everybody's pumping and drilling out in Taft!"

"Hmmm…well, when I visited your guys out in Taft recently, they told me that the most important thing to them was having the right inventory on hand when they needed it. We would like to explore how we can help solve this problem for you, because it seems to be just as important as cost. We can simplify the ordering process at the very least, which will make the shipping process go a lot faster. But given our financial situation, we really can't offer a price cut right now."

"Or we can just go to a new supplier! What do you think of that?" Ray responded.

Oh, great, thought Robert. *He's pulling the ol' "We can get this somewhere else cheaper and faster" line.*

"Well," Robert said, "You can, but it would really be to your disadvantage, to be honest. For being a great, loyal customer, OPF makes specialty products for Braemar, and if you switch to a new supplier now, your company will have to work to get these products developed and manufactured. This will take time away from developing your new oil fields. Plus, we are in the process of co-design on several pieces of new equipment, as you may know. Our engineers are working closely with yours."

Ray sheepishly admitted that this was true. "Okay," Ray said. "We have actually talked about this internally. Our switching costs could be as much as $3 million. However, some of your competitors are coming up with new technologies that appear to be very attractive. If we can't get the price down for OPF products, we will have to look at the alternatives."

Robert continued, "Why don't we come back to this conversation after we've both thought about it for a bit? I'll give you a call later this week."

He quickly ended the meeting there before he became angry. He knew where he wanted to go with this deal and was anxious to get back to his office to start drafting up the CNAs, trades and MEOs.

Consequences of No Agreement (CNAs)

Once Robert was back at his desk, he drafted a list of CNAs for both sides.

OPF's side (Vendor):

- Loss of $24 million in annual revenue
- Loss of major customer

- Customer is long-time partner of OPF, and a friend (there are emotions involved)
- Further in debt; possibly no chance of pulling out of bankruptcy

Braemar's side (Buyer):

- Transition to another supplier = $3 million
  - Cost of change and may take up to six months to transition all of the parts
- Fear of the unknown if they go to a different supplier
- Cost of developing required specialty products
- Loss of time in developing their new drilling fields
- Damaged relationship with OPF

Robert's list of CNAs clearly identified OPF as having greater economic loss. Not only would they lose $24 million in annual revenue, losing Braemar would mean it would be so much harder to climb out of bankruptcy. Although Braemar would lose approximately $3 million by transitioning to a different supplier, a bigger loss to them would be time. They would lose time in developing their new drilling fields and in waiting for their new supplier to become familiar with their wants and needs (especially their specialty products). Robert thought that he could play up this issue, as Braemar was anxious to begin development on their new fields.

Creating and Dividing Value

Using what he knew about Braemar, Robert drafted a list of potential trades for each side. Of course, he wanted to create a better solution for the deal but he had to be careful that the trades that he was going to offer Braemar weren't going to be too much of a cost burden on OPF. He was looking for things of small value to OPF, but big value to Braemar.

OPF's potential trades:
- Discount: three to five percent
- Simplified ordering process (probably worth about $50K annually in time and effort to Braemar)
- Dedicated account manager
- Monthly usage and inventory analysis to make sure that they are stocking the most critical parts at all times
- 24/7 support center access
- More access to engineering to co-develop new products

Braemar's potential trades:
- Longer-term blanket contract that they release against (five years)
- Dedicating 90 percent of all their pipe and fitting business to OPF (up from 75 percent)
- Access to other Braemar divisions in Texas, Louisiana, Indonesia, Malaysia
- Product development staff and Marketing staff to drive new products

When writing up his list of trades, Robert kept in mind the importance of creating value for each side. He knew that this was essential to convincing Braemar that a price discount was not the only valuable thing on the table. Each side had areas of interest to each other; it was just a matter of taking those areas and developing them into valuable and beneficial opportunities for each party.

Robert knew that this wasn't just a simple case of selling to Braemar. He also had to coordinate with OPF Purchasing and Production Scheduling to get the raw material vendors in line and with manufacturing to get the right inventory produced at the right time. He would also have to plan for more inventory on hand for the frequently used parts to improve field response time. This was a bigger supply chain challenge than he had anticipated. It was going to take major shifts in the way OPF planned for and managed inventory. But better inventory management would be very valuable to Braemar, and cost OPF some investment in more inventory and a revision to the inventory management process. Inventory was a big deal for Purchasing. They were constantly being criticized for not having the raw materials delivered on time to manufacturing and Production would blame them for delays in finishing products. Robert knew he would have to work on these processes eventually, too. Inventory was a two-edged sword and affected multiple business operations.

This was just the kind of big, meaty project that Robert loved to work on. Perhaps he could help design some new procurement, manufacturing and inventory processes at OPF that would make a big difference in the way they operated and served customers. He got excited thinking about the possibilities of expanding OPF's relationship with Braemar. Using his list of trades as a foundation, he moved on to drafting a few MEOs for the deal.

Identifying Multiple Equal Offers (MEOs)

Below is a chart of three different offers that Robert was to propose to Braemar.

Robert's Braemar Offers

Field Advantage	Fast Response	Business as Usual
5% discount	3% discount	2% discount
5 year contract	3 year contract	3 year contract
24/7 access to customer service	Simplified ordering process	
Simplified ordering process	Shared inventory information	
OPF-managed inventory in the field	Quarterly business reviews	
Braemar has access to OPF engineering for new product development	90% business commitment	
Quarterly Business Reviews		
Intro to other Braemar divisions		

Negotiation Results

Robert and Ray met the following week to re-negotiate their contract and talk more about their situation. Robert wanted to ease into the renegotiation conversation but Ray, obviously anxious to squeeze a discount out of OPF, dove right into the topic. Skipping pleasantries, he immediately asked Robert if he thought any differently about giving Braemar a price cut. Robert knew that there was a high chance that Ray was going to act like this, so he had prepared for it that morning. He had the details of his MEOs all memorized and carefully went through each with Ray, beginning with the one that he deemed least appealing, "Business as Usual." He began with this one because he wanted to have the other offers sound better and better to Ray as he explained them. In Robert's mind, "Field Advantage" offer was the best on his list because both parties benefited greatly from its components. But any of the offers were in the Agreement Zone between the two companies and would be acceptable. After going through each one of the offers, Ray started to mellow. They took a quick break for coffee and resumed their discussion.

Ray agreed that the "Field Advantage" offer was the best and he was very interested in the trades. Apparently, Braemar was very interested in developing several new products, but didn't have the engineering staff to do it. "Field Advantage" solved that problem. He also liked the idea of Quarterly Business Reviews. That way he could keep the pressure on OPF to come up with new ideas. And with this deal, Braemar also got the price discount they wanted!

Epilogue

The negotiations continued between Robert and Ray, and ultimately they signed a new contract detailing "Field Advantage" even further. Although Ray had anchored OPF at a five percent discount, Robert found a way to make the terms acceptable. A five-year contract meant that OPF's bank would be willing to lend them more working capital. Robert continued on finding ways to secure OPF's future and release the company from bankruptcy.

Next, Robert called the Purchasing staff together to tell them about the deal and ask that they try to get an additional three to five percent discount from each of their vendors. But before they did this, he was sending them all to Strategic Negotiation training. Now he knew for sure how valuable the Think! methodology was for the OPF business.

Lessons Learned

This was the second deal in which Robert had used the Think! Inc. Strategic Negotiation methodology. From the previous case, he had learned that creating and dividing joint value for both parties was important. He applied the same concept here and succeeded. Although Robert had to provide a price discount to Braemar, he gained much more financially in the long-term and developed a somewhat positive relationship with Ray, which also benefitted the company in the long-run.

- MEOs soften the tough negotiations and give vendors and customers acceptable options to consider
- Talking with a customer or vendor about their needs is a way of validating CNAs and discovering trades
- Field trips to operating locations can be real eye-openers and will help to clarify what is really important in a deal
- Even though one party may be stuck on cost, by developing trades, you can change the conversation

Case Study #6 – Baumans Co. & Premier Works

"Aggregating Demand"

Situation Overview and Business Problem

Baumans Co. had an array of services for their clients. They specialized in face-to-face marketing and events—specifically, their primary service was creating trade show displays for various businesses and companies. Baumans' clients came to them with varying levels of preparation, ideas and trade show experience; sometimes they knew exactly what they wanted and sometimes they hadn't the slightest idea. It was the company's job to help them plan for their event—everything from graphics design to program management— and execute it to a T.

Creating trade show displays was a unique niche industry and it wasn't exactly a recession-proof trade. When the global economy was in a precarious state and companies typically cut their trade show budgets to save money, Baumans suffered the consequences.

Baumans was a job shop environment, which meant that they produced their services in one-off production or in relatively low numbers throughout the year. Typically, "trade show seasons" were Spring and Fall so they experienced a peak in business in the Summer and Winter as companies prepared for shows. Business hadn't exactly plummeted during the recession but it wasn't at an all-time high either. However, the Sales team had done a fairly effective job with promotion the last couple of years as they emphasized to their customers the importance of increased market share through trade show advertising. Still, many companies only saw the crisis that was rapidly unfolding in the global economic downturn and they subsequently cut their marketing and advertising budgets, including funds for trade show booth construction and graphics.

Despite these external events, Carrie Tannenbaum, Baumans' Purchasing Manager, was uncertain about how things were going with the company. The company, being in such a unique industry, wasn't in any deep financial trouble even though the future was very unsure. After all, how long could an organization creating trade show displays last in such a volatile environment? After trying to come up with creative ways to save on expenses, she turned her attention to other ideas in which the company could reduce spending.

Baumans offered many products and services and Carrie planned a new attack strategy: identify the top three common commodities for all transactions for the past five years. She was hoping that she would be able to bundle those common commodities/services together for a volume discount with one or more of the vendors. After her research, Carrie discovered that in almost every transaction, clients needed furnishing, audio and visual and graphics in their booths. Baumans' contract with their audio and visual vendor, Premier Works, was up for re-negotiation. Almost every transaction performed within the last five years needed some type of audio and visual product and/or service so Carrie assumed that almost every future transaction would need this service as well. Carrie thought that this information would be very beneficial for Premier since it meant that Premier would be involved in practically every Baumans job. It was the perfect time for Carrie to ask Premier for a discount.

As Purchasing Manager, her primary focus was saving money. But focusing only on price went against the very core of strategic negotiating. She knew that price was never the only item in a negotiation, and she was going to have to trade for some things in order to get the best value for Baumans. Carrie also knew she needed to create an acceptable deal for the vendor, too.

Consequences of No Agreement (CNAs)

Carrie began to mull over the CNAs of the situation. What would happen if she and Premier couldn't come to an agreement? What were the alternatives to making this deal? Carrie thought about the CNAs for both parties involved. In fact, she remembered that she needed to determine Premier's CNA so she would know how to define an Agreement Zone where a deal would work for both Baumans and Premier. There was no use in pushing beyond their CNA, she remembered, because Premier would never agree and might just walk away.

No, she thought, *I have to keep the deal within the Agreement Zone... but I still want to grab as much of the value as I can. So, what would be our CNA and their CNA if we don't do this deal?*

CNA – Buyer's side (Baumans):

- No savings (she was hoping for 15–20 percent discount or about $2 million/yr)
- Loss of key, long-term vendor for most transactions/clients
- Tough transition to new vendor
- Disruption in service
- Long learning curve for new vendor

CNA – Seller's side (Premier):

- Loss of major customer
  - Replace lost business with new customer
  - Get more business from existing customer
- Loss of 25 percent of revenue—$15 million/year
- Loss of business reputation
- Loss of strategic partnership
- Loss of good buyer-seller relationship with great customer

The details of both CNA lists brought to light the fact that both Baumans and Premier had a lot to lose. We'd better get this deal done. I should also start thinking about developing a second supplier, just in case something goes wrong with the negotiations or with the relationship in the future, thought Carrie.

Identifying Anchors

Carrie knew from her training that there were two types of anchors: opening offers and other anchors. She was already set on anchoring on a 25 percent price discount from Premier, with ultimately getting at least 20 percent. She was going to explain that Baumans' customers were also cutting their budgets and negotiating more discounted pricing. She planned to plant the price discount anchor in the negotiation early. Carrie wanted to use this as the top component of all three of her MEOs; hopefully, one of the options would appeal to Premier and she would be able to finalize the deal.

Identifying and Dividing Value

The main thing on her mind was price. But she knew that the best negotiations included a variety of different items, such as price, length of agreement, service, payment terms, legal terms and volume that represented different values and different priorities to each party.[12] And there were other things of value to be traded, too. She recalled that strategic trades were also known as "Level 3 Trades."

After taking a first pass at determining both parties' CNAs and settling on her anchor, Carrie called Premier's Sales department and arranged an in-person meeting with their Sales Manager, John Strong. This meeting was to confirm her CNA estimations for Premier and to discuss possible trade options and priorities for their deal.

Carrie knew that Baumans had a solid working relationship with Premier. Premier had been providing audio and visual products and services for Baumans for the last five years and Carrie didn't want to be the one to screw things up. She was determined to be amicable during their meeting, no matter what the outcome. Luckily, she had worked with John before, and Carrie remembered that he was quite pleasant to do business with.

— — —

Carrie and John met over lunch the following week. They discussed the situation for over an hour; Carrie explained what was going on with Baumans' (casually signaling her CNAs) and detailed how going into a new contract with a price discount could benefit both companies, not just Baumans. John was very empathetic as he made it clear how detrimental losing Baumans would be to his company. Carrie confirmed the fact that Premier was one of Baumans' best suppliers and she strongly expressed her interest in continuing their relationship.

In light of Premier's support, John and Carrie were able to briefly broach the topic of potential trades. The meeting was going along so well that she thought that she might as well try and obtain more useful

---

[12] Brian J. Dietmeyer with Rob Kaplan, 17.

information from John. Since he was determined not to lose Baumans as a customer, he was totally open to the idea of trading items that would benefit both companies. In addition to a possible price discount, John offered Carrie a few more services that Premier would be willing to provide, if Baumans could offer a longer-term contract, access to online ordering systems, and information on trends within the trade show industry.

The meeting couldn't have gone better—not only did Carrie receive support from John, she was glad to see that her approach was working. Preparing the CNAs beforehand really drove the meeting discussion; it made her and John more aware of the seriousness of the situation and more prepared for developing trades. As soon as Carrie returned to her office, she reviewed her notes from the meeting and drafted a list of both companies' potential trades. John, understanding the importance of "expanding the pie" (i.e., identifying more items for trade in order to create more value for both sides to divide), had graciously offered several services that he'd be willing to offer in the negotiation. Carrie also threw in a few more that she decided to keep in her back pocket if she needed them during the next meeting. Here are the lists she came up with after reviewing her meeting notes:

Baumans' potential trades:
- Longer-term contract: three to five years
- Access to online ordering systems—could provide one head count in savings to Premier to be able to automate the ordering process
- Access to user group with Baumans' customers
- New technology ideas and the opportunity for Premier to bid on them
- Joint research project for trends in the trade show industry
- Joint presentation at next trade show industry event

Premier's potential trades:

- Price reduction: seven to 10 percent
- On-site service at trade shows for no additional charge
- New technology seminars for Baumans' employees
- Employee discount extended to Baumans' employees for high-tech equipment

Identifying Multiple Equal Offers (MEOs)

After validating Premier's CNAs and developing Wish List estimations (i.e., potential trades) for both parties, Carrie felt that she had a good handle on the situation. There was no doubt as to whether or not Premier wanted to continue doing business with Baumans; John had reiterated that fact many times during their meeting. Now she had to make sure to come up with solutions that created joint value and that provided both parties with deals that were greater than their CNAs.[13]

Carrie began with the goal of the negotiation. Her goal was to receive a price reduction from Premier. Premier's goal was to continue their business relationship with Baumans; in other words, their goal was to have Baumans sign a longer contract. These two points would be definite items in all three MEOs. Using this as a starting point, she outlined her MEOs, making sure to embed information from the CNAs and potential trade lists of both companies:

Carrie's Premier/Baumans MEOs

Continuing Business	Good Business	Strategic Partnership
3% discount across the board	10% discount across the board	10% discount on existing products; 5% discount on new technology
1 year contract with 1 year renewal options	3 year contract with 1 year renewal options	3 year contract with 1 year renewal options
On-site trade show service	On-site trade show service	On-site trade show service

---

[13] Ibid., 133.

Carrie's Premier/Baumans MEOs (continued)

Continuing Business	Good Business	Strategic Partnership
	Joint research project on trade show trends	Joint research project on trade show trends
	Online ordering system access	Online ordering system access
		New technology seminars
		Baumans user group access

Carrie purposely left off a couple of items that were in the lists of potential trades, just in case they came in handy later. Despite that, she was confident in her MEOs. She called John and arranged another in-person meeting to discuss these options.

Negotiation Results

Carrie and John met within the next week. After pleasantries and casual small talk, they both felt comfortable discussing Carrie's MEOs. She laid out her chart on the table and went through each option carefully. Each option looked better than the next, as she purposely added more beneficial items with each alternative solution. She was hoping that the third option, "Strategic Partnership," would look the most appealing to John as it included many of Baumans' and Premier's Wish List items. Overall, John was impressed with Carrie's efforts but felt like there were still more items for trade.

"I would love to go with 'Strategic Partnership,'" he said. "But, I bet we could do better. What else can we do to make this new partnership feel like a partnership? Is there something else that we can do together that would benefit the both of us?"

Carrie was glad that she was prepared.

"Well, with the 'Strategic Partnership' option, since we're going to be working together on researching trade show trends, technology seminars and user groups, why don't we do something together in public? To show our customers and target markets that we're working jointly to better our services to them?"

"What do you have in mind?" asked John.

"For the next trade show industry event, why doesn't Premier join us?" said Carrie. "We can work on a presentation together where we can showcase our research results, new technologies, how companies who choose Baumans for their next trade show would benefit greatly because we have a great partnership with our electrical vendor...you know, hype it up a bit."

"That sounds absolutely wonderful! Great idea to present our partnership to the public like that."

With that, Carrie and John finalized the details of their new agreement and had their new contract written up within the next couple of weeks.

Epilogue

Over the next three years, the new partnership proved to be quite beneficial for Baumans and Premier. Baumans had early access to information about Premier's new technologies during their seminars, which their joint research with Baumans on trade show trends only helped to develop. Baumans' customers were also happy with the new partnership as they felt more comfortable contacting and communicating with Premier on any technology issues. It was a true joint value situation and it became a no-brainer for the two companies to renew their contract every time it came up for renewal.

Lessons Learned

Although Carrie's ultimate goal was to obtain a price reduction, she utilized Think! Inc.'s Strategic Negotiation methodology to receive more out of the situation. She was lucky to have an honest business relationship with her vendor. This proved to be highly advantageous as Carrie was able to work with John in creating the best solution possible for both companies.

Case Study #7 – Pershing Auto Parts & Value Electric

"Disaster Happens"

Situation Overview and Business Problem

At Pershing Auto Parts, Charles Birrell sat slumped in his office chair. He was on his third cup of coffee and it was barely 9:00 a.m. Despite that, he was exhausted. Being the Purchasing Manager of an automotive supplier was a tough position with the current state of the U.S. economy and the last several years had definitely taken their toll on him. Charles always felt mentally drained; no good news ever seemed to be generated by the auto industry anymore and it didn't seem to be getting any better. Like his customers, he had lost faith. But unlike his customers, he *had* to invest all of his efforts in the industry because his job depended on it. He was in his late-50s and if he lost his job, he would pretty much be forced into retirement.

Charles slid further back in his chair and daydreamed about the good old days when the auto industry was a symbol of American dominance and pride, instead of a symbol of American decline. He had been working in this industry for 30 plus years and it depressed him to see what it had become. He was sick of hearing about, and personally experiencing, layoffs and plant shutdowns. The industry had somehow become reliant on these short-term attempts to save money; the desperation was so tangible that he couldn't help feeling useless. Although it helped to get Pershing's expenses down, the unfortunate side effect was the immediate decrease in employee morale. Now you had to pay for coffee in the break room, be careful how many copies you made and empty your own trash can every day. Workers no longer felt stable in their jobs and this undermined the company's long-term performance. Charles did what he could, though, and began to mull over his workload.

Currently, his most pressing problem at Pershing was the company's relationship with their electrical vendor, Value Electric. Pershing's COO was pressuring Charles to squeeze a 15 percent discount out of Value Electric since they could no longer afford to pay the current price levels. Their contract was up for re-negotiation and Pershing desperately needed a price cut. Pershing primarily manufactured robotics for automotive assembly lines (e.g., starters and batteries) so a big part of the company's spending money went towards electronics for their robots.

The company had seen a gradual downturn in orders since 2008 and Charles didn't have cause to believe that it would improve any time within the next few months. Reduced orders and auto manufacturing affected the entire auto industry, not just Pershing. No, it seemed like the only solution was to get Value Electric to agree to their suggested 15 percent price discount. Charles knew that it was a hefty amount that they were asking but Pershing was up against the wall here. It wasn't just the large discount that Charles dreaded asking for. He had actually re-negotiated their contract with Value last year where they were pretty much in the same boat. Charles asked for a five percent discount then and ultimately ended up with three percent. That was a miracle last year but now the company's funds were even scarcer—how in the world was he going to get Value to agree to 15 percent?

Pershing had sent the Purchasing department to a negotiations workshop last year and Charles was an avid user of blueprinting the negotiation. Over the past 20 years, he had gotten vendors to concede to price cuts by persistently asking them (and adding a little bit of guilt-trip-ping). But since so much was riding on the success of this renegotiation, and because he had already asked Value Electric last year for a price discount, Charles didn't feel comfortable with pressuring Value for a price reduction alone. Now seemed like the best time to try something creative.

Investigating and Validating the Problem

The first step of the process was for Charles to estimate the CNAs for both sides. Before delving into that, however, Charles wanted to think through the problem. It was obvious that Pershing wasn't in good financial standing; he had been at the company for far too long to not understand that.

Within the last five years, Pershing had to lay off about half of the company and conducted one to two plant shutdowns a year. The dip in sales trended with the economic downturn, and with it went company morale. Charles lost any luster or enthusiasm he once had for the auto industry and the sales numbers he was currently poring over didn't make him feel any better. It was daunting how much sales had declined just within the last year and although it was discouraging, Charles felt that showing Value Electric these numbers would help persuade them to concede to Pershing's 15 percent price discount.

It wasn't like Value Electric wasn't aware of Pershing's dire financial situation, though. With General Motors taking loan guarantees from the government and the recent decreasing sales of European automobiles, the decline of the American auto industry was globally known. It seemed like all U.S. auto-makers, and all other businesses tied to auto-making (e.g., auto suppliers like Pershing), were on the brink of falling into bankruptcy. Over the years, General Motors, Chrysler and Ford had all forced their suppliers, including Pershing, to make price concessions. Now, in an attempt to save itself, Pershing had to do the same to its suppliers including Value Electric.

Consequences of No Agreement (CNAs)

Charles knew the problem with Pershing was money. The company's declining sales, number of layoffs and plant shutdowns, and every piece of auto news out there confirmed it. He would have no problem convincing Value Electric that this was strictly an economic issue and Value Electric needed to help them respond to it by providing a price concession.

Knowing this, Charles then turned his attention over to estimating the CNAs. He took out a pen and quickly wrote up a list in his notebook.

What would the consequences be for Pershing if they didn't get the price discount?

Buyer's side:

- No savings—company must cut internal costs further, more lay-offs or possibly bankruptcy
- Competitor empowerment (especially if their competitors were getting price concessions from their own vendors)
- Transition to another supplier
- Potential loss of business to competitors

What would the consequences be for Value if they didn't provide the price concession?

Seller's side:

- Loss of major customer—approximately $20 million in lost revenue
- Potential for making zero margin on sales
- Competitor empowerment

Is this right? Should they be longer lists? Charles thought to himself. Charles racked his brain for more CNAs to jot down but he came up with nothing. Giving up, he moved on to identifying anchors for the deal. He would start with a 20 percent discount anchor with the hopes of settling on 15 percent. *Wow!* he thought. This was going to be a stretch.

Identifying and Dividing Value

Next up was estimating the list of potential trades for each side. Charles remembered that the workshop stressed the importance of creating value, which makes trading items possible. Aside from a longer contract, Charles knew of a few more things that Pershing could offer Value Electric (keeping Pershing's scarce funding in mind, he made sure that they were items that didn't cost much for Pershing but would be valuable for Value Electric). He outlined each side's potential trades:

Pershing's potential trades:

- Longer contract five to seven years with options to renew
- Access to other divisions of Pershing including the new China operations
- White papers/referrals to other industry colleagues
- Joint product development

Value's potential trades:

- Price concession (at least 15 percent)
- Extended warranty one to two years
- Improved customer service
  - Increased phone support 24/7

Identifying Anchors

Charles rethought his anchoring strategy. He decided to go with his initial anchor of a price discount of 20 percent. Obviously, it was steep, especially since he was only able to negotiate a measly three percent last year. But he had to try.

Feeling anxious about the precarious state of their contract in general, Charles picked up the phone and called George Barba, the President of Value Electric. After some forced pleasantries, Charles said what was on his mind.

"So, George… as you know, Pershing isn't doing so well and our contract with Value Electric is coming to an end. We're going to have to re-negotiate sooner or later and I was hoping I could talk to you about a price discount."

An imperceptibly long, awkward pause proceeded as this lingered in the air.

"… What exactly are you thinking of?" George finally asked, albeit reluctantly.

"Something in the neighborhood of 17 to 20 percent," Charles said.

"Ha! You've got to be kidding, right? You know we already gave you a three percent discount last year, right?? We're having the same exact conversation. You promised that Pershing was going to try and improve volumes for us and that never happened. Now you're asking for a 17 to 20 percent discount?"

"I know it's a lot…but we're in deep trouble here. If this wasn't absolutely necessary, I wouldn't be asking. I also made this list of things that may be of additional value to you. For example, we can discuss Value Electric having access to Pershing's other divisions, including China; white papers/referrals; joint product development…and in exchange, you should consider the discount, maybe even an extended warranty…"

"Ha ha! This is ridiculous. What makes you think that we're going to give you other things in *addition* to a large price discount? Like you said, Pershing's in the hole; why would Value Electric invest more in a company that's not doing well? Your business is important to us, but also very risky."

"Well, what would happen if you didn't give us the discount and you lost our business?" Charles blurted.

"That is a very good question, Charles. One that I can definitely answer. We would go to different customers, simple as that. One that won't ask us for a price that would drive us into bankruptcy, too. Perhaps we'd scale back our business and sell to other industries. You know what, I don't want to talk about this anymore; I'm getting too angry and I might say some things I'll regret. We'll talk later."

George hung up and left Charles on the other end with his self-confidence gone.

Identifying Multiple Equal Offers (MEOs)

Although the phone call with George didn't go as planned, Charles was determined to persist. He had already estimated the CNAs and trades; now it was time to make a chart outlining his Multiple Equal Offers (MEOs).

There was no way Pershing could leave the deal without some sort of discount to stay in business so he wasn't giving up on that. He began with the 15 percent discount and created two more options outlining items with a 16 and 17 percent discount.

Helping Each Other	Medium Range Business	Rebuilding our Health
15% discount	16% discount	17% discount
1 year contract	3 year contract	5 year contract with 2 year extension option
	Up to 5 referrals	Extended warranty
		Joint product development
		Improved phone support

Negotiation Results

A few days after Charles and George's heated phone conversation, Charles called the President of Value Electric to try again. The recent phone call was definitely discouraging but Charles knew he couldn't give up without giving Value multiple options. He was determined to prove to George that they could come to an agreement.

"No price cut, Charles," George said as he picked up the phone.

Not a good sign already, thought Charles.

"How'd you know it was me?" he asked, baffled.

"Caller ID. Keep up, Charles," George remarked sharply.

"Hm. Well, George, I know our last phone conversation ended badly but I've been thinking about our options and I'd like to arrange a face-to-face meeting so we can discuss them," said Charles.

"What makes you think that meeting in-person will make me say 'yes'?"

"Come on, we'll meet for lunch. I'll show you what I've been thinking about and I'm sure that we can meet in the middle."

After a long pause (George was good at making Charles feel awkward and uncertain with these dramatic pauses), George agreed to fly out to Detroit.

— — —

George was able to obtain a flight to Detroit for the next day, but asked for a meeting at Pershing, not at lunch. The meeting started in the vendor conference room at 10 a.m. George wasn't interested in pleasantries and tiptoeing around the situation at hand, which forced Charles to present his MEOs to him immediately. He pulled out his MEO chart that he had outlined several days ago.

"*This* is what you've been working on? *This* is what you wanted to show me? These are Value's options?? I told you that we weren't going to go for a price discount and although I appreciate you aiming high, this is unacceptable. You don't even give me an option for a lower price concession! These are 15 percent and higher!" George exclaimed, raising his voice.

"And I told you that we just cannot do the deal without a price discount. 15 percent is the discount rate we must achieve," Charles stated.

"I'm sorry, then. This was a total waste of time. Not only can I not give you a price concession, I'm afraid Value Electric won't be able to work with Pershing any longer," George replied matter-of-factly as he began to get up.

"Thanks but no thanks." And with that, George walked out before Charles could stop him.

Epilogue

Charles was devastated. He had lost a long-time Pershing supplier in less than an hour. He was dreading breaking the news to his boss. He slowly walked back to his office. On the way there, he made a decision to give the COO his two-week notice. Although Pershing hadn't been doing great these last several years, Charles was a practical person when it came to his personal finances and saving money. With all the layoffs that occurred, he knew that there was a high chance that he could be without a job someday, so he saved every penny he could and never made any extravagant purchases. He walked into his boss's office, explained what had just happened during his meeting with Value Electric, gave his notice, and walked out of the office feeling relieved, even a bit giddy.

Pershing had given him a lot the past 30 plus years but he was already putting it all behind him.

Lessons Learned

Charles made many mistakes. Creating a better solution for both parties involved is the goal and in order to do that, Charles should have better identified Value Electric's CNA and the Agreement Zone. In this case, Value Electric chose their alternative—to walk away. Value Electric walked away from the deal because Pershing was not offering a deal better than their alternative. The two companies just could not come to terms.

When Charles spoke to George to confirm Value Electric's CNAs and potential trades (i.e., Wish List), he should have listened more carefully. Value was not prepared to accept further discounting, no matter what. At that point, Charles should have started negotiations with an alternate vendor.

Case Study #8 – Universal Electronics Smartphone Cameras

"A Picture's Worth a Thousand Words"

Situation Overview and Business Problem

The third generation of Universal Electronics Inc.'s popular line of smartphones, Skarp, was currently in the works. It had been about two years since Universal, headquartered in Silicon Valley, released the Skarp 2 and its sales had made Universal one of the top three smartphone manufacturers in the world. The new version of Skarp (Skarp 3) was going to have a slew of improvements from their last version; in addition to being thinner and faster, it was also going to have a better quality camera, better cell phone reception and be a more receptive hotspot for wireless Internet connections.

Developing and creating Skarp 3 was a complex global supply chain process. The design and specifications were done in Silicon Valley. Universal purchased the phone's many components from various subcontracted companies around the world, and engaged a well-known contract manufacturer in Guangzhou, China to do the final assembly. Smartphones were getting better in quality and Universal had to keep up with the rapid pace of technological advances to keep the phone buyers interested in Skarp. Universal was competing against other popular smartphone manufacturers and one of the things that lured customers into purchasing Skarps was the high quality cameras. Universal wanted Skarp 3's cameras to be faster than their last version and to take sharper, more hi-res photos. That was one of the key improvements of the new Skarp 3 version, and Universal wanted to make sure that they were going to get quality camera components from their electronics manufacturer, Packer Co.

Manufacturing in Shenzhen, China, Packer was a multinational company that designed and made tiny electronic cameras for many laptop and smartphone companies around the world. They had worked with Universal before, manufacturing the cameras for the previous two generations of Skarp. Alex Tsao, the Sales Manager at Packer, was currently working with Sanjiv Malik, Universal's Purchasing Commodity Manager, at Universal's headquarters in Silicon Valley.

The Universal campus was always abuzz with activity. The company's public image was one of spectacular innovation; the Founder and

CEO continually encouraged new ideas and this creativity was evident in their products. Skarp 3 was set to be released soon and the entire company was working around the clock to perfect its design. As the Purchasing Commodity Manager for cameras at Universal, Sanjiv was responsible for obtaining the new phone's top quality cameras. Universal was closely monitoring and pushing production schedules as they were attempting to coordinate multiple different manufacturers for various components of the phone.

Demand for Skarp 3 was high—Universal was forecasting sales of two million phones in the first month. Sanjiv was expected to negotiate a low price for the cameras. Every Commodity Manager was under pressure to reduce component costs in order to keep the overall cost of the finished product competitive with other phones on the market. Demand for higher quality cameras was also increasing as competing smartphone competitors were working on improving their products' cameras.

This was unfortunate for both Universal and Packer as Packer was struggling with production. Packer had been unable to achieve the quality demanded by Universal. Packer's production yield rates for the quality requirements for cameras were too low. The only way to improve the quality and the production yield rates was by implementing an expensive new process that added cost to production. Packer engineers saw no other way to improve the quality yield rates. Packer had to increase the cameras' price to all of their smartphone customers, not just Universal, to recover from the increased manufacturing costs.

Sanjiv and Alex had been discussing the camera transaction since Universal began developing Skarp 3. Months ago, to plant the seed early and anchor the discount, Sanjiv had mentioned that Universal would probably need a three to five percent price discount. Alex Tsao countered by signaling that the price for the cameras was increasing proportionately to the increase in the cost of quality production in accordance with Universal's new specifications. The problem was fairly simple: product quality improves, price goes up. In order to obtain the expected product cost that Skarp 3 required, however, Sanjiv had to try and lower its price point significantly. Stalemate!

To each other's detriment and frustration, both Sanjiv and Alex were at opposite ends of the deal spectrum. They had both explained their thought processes for their decisions several times to each other and while it made sense for Packer to raise their price and for Universal to want a discount, Sanjiv and Alex didn't seem to want to compromise. It was just like Republicans and Democrats in Congress!

Sanjiv discussed the situation with his manager, Mason Pulliam, who mentioned a new methodology that might help. The Senior Purchasing and Senior Sales Management had recently attended a pilot workshop on Strategic Negotiation, where they were taught how business negotiation was an analytical process with rational steps and measureable, improvable results.

Sanjiv took careful notes during the conversation with his manager but his stubbornness got in the way of wanting to try the process on the Packer negotiation. Mason insisted that he try the process. Sanjiv's manager gave him the class booklet on the methodology. The rationale behind each step was logical and easy to understand but having never used the process first-hand, Sanjiv was unsure of how it would play out and how confident he would be when negotiating with Alex. Still, he had to try because his boss instructed him to do so. Mason was actively coaching him so that soothed his nerves some. Using case study examples and hypothetical deals from *Strategic Negotiation*, Sanjiv and Mason began blueprinting the Packer negotiation, starting with identifying each side's CNA. Together, they white-boarded the CNAs for both sides.

Consequences of No Agreement (CNAs)

Buyer's side (Universal):

- Late product launch (this would be completely unacceptable to Universal and Sanjiv could be fired if the product was delayed due to cameras)
  - Delayed sales and thus delayed or lost revenue of hundreds of millions of launch dollars
  - Loss of competitive positioning for Universal

- Loss of business reputation
- Transition to another supplier
  - Development time up to six months
  - Long learning curve for new vendor
- Loss of key vendor that is familiar with product and has delivered in the past

Seller's side (Packer):
- Loss of at least $102 million in annual sales
- Loss of reputation for camera production
- Loss of major brand customer
- Having to publically announce the loss of this customer due to SEC reporting requirements

Identifying Anchors

The CNA estimations had yet to be validated by Packer but even if one or two of them were off, it was still evident that both sides were very heavily invested in the transaction and had a lot to lose. If the companies could not come to any agreement and Universal lost Packer as a vendor, it meant a late product launch as they worked to transition to a new supplier. This would force them to fall behind their competitors; the public would most likely lose interest by the time of Skarp 3's release, especially if Universal's competitors had already unveiled their new phones.

Because of this, Sanjiv was determined to set an anchor first. He wanted to put it plainly on the table that Universal needed at least a five percent discount from Packer in addition to on-time delivery. Mason agreed that they needed to open with the first offer but he disagreed with Sanjiv's planned approach.

"Since you and Alex have been in talks about this for a while, he already knows that we need a discount. There's no point in setting an anchor with already established information. We need to word it in such a way where we imply how much we need the price discount, but include a 'Here's what's in it for you, too' point."

"How do we do that?"

"When we have the meeting with Alex, we'll discuss our CNAs as well as Packer's CNAs. Ideally, this conversation will allow us to validate and learn more about the items on their priority list (i.e., their potential trades). Thus, we'll be sharing and trading information. Hopefully, the meeting goes well and both companies will benefit. So, instead of just saying, 'Universal cannot pay more than $X per camera and therefore needs a five percent discount,' we should say something like 'We are anticipating a very high demand for Skarp 3 and in order to give our customers what they want, when they want it, and ensure that we have enough product in stock, we need a lower price point for these cameras. I know keeping the price point high is important to you, though, and we understand that you need to do this in order to achieve our quality requirements. But, how important is it to you to have a customer that is producing one of the most popular (and lucrative) technological products today? How important is it to you to keep partnering with us, possibly even help us with developing new products?' See, Sanjiv, this way we say several different things. We're saying that we are one of the most popular smartphone manufacturers (thus, putting us in a better position than some of our other competitors) and we get to work in an item that we're willing to trade with them (assisting with developing new products)."

"And what are these trades exactly?"

"I'll show you— we'll work together on them. These things are what is going to be most appealing to Alex and Packer. Trades are items that have different values for us and them, and ultimately create joint value solutions out of negotiations. Like I said, talking with them to validate their CNAs will allow us to learn more about what is valuable to them."

Identifying and Dividing Value

Sanjiv arranged a meeting with Alex for the next day. The purpose of this meeting was to learn more about Packer's CNAs and to get Alex to share some information. Mason had met Alex before so he knew how obstinate Alex could be when he had already made up his mind. Sanjiv was relieved that Mason was coaching him through this entire deal, as he knew that his own stubbornness sometimes hindered progress.

Overall, the meeting was amicable and provided a lot of valuable information. Sanjiv discussed their CNAs and asked questions to validate his estimated CNAs for Packer. Mason placed their opening anchor on the table by asking the question that he discussed with Sanjiv the day before. Alex confirmed that although he was not able to provide a high price discount, he wanted to keep working with Universal because of their popularity and capability to reach other markets globally. Of course, Alex was also thinking about his commission on the deal. There was no way he was going to lose the Universal account.

Sanjiv and Mason were glad to hear Alex say this and they shared information about other items and services that each company had and was willing to offer as part of the deal. After the meeting, Sanjiv and Mason returned to their Universal offices and white-boarded each side's list of potential trades based on the information from their meeting. Wanting to expand the pie, they included as many valuable, tradable items as they could.

Universal's potential trades:

- Keep contract as is—no discount, and no increase (although they could approve up to two percent increase if this was commiserate with the increase in quality)
- Payable days reduced from N45 to N30
- Introduction to Universal's new product development teams for other products (e.g., laptops, digital assistants)
- Identification on Universal's website as one of Universal's approved and primary vendors

Packer's potential trades:

- Keep contract as is in exchange for increase in volume by 10–15 percent for other products
- Two to three R&D engineers on loan to Universal for development of next-gen cameras for Skarp 4

- 24/7 second-level technical assistance if customers have trouble with the cameras on Skarp 3

Identifying Multiple Equal Offers (MEOs)

Using their priority list trade estimations as a foundation, Sanjiv and Mason then drafted three MEOs, identifying the Level 3 trades as the most strategic, creative and beneficial.

Status Quo	Refresh Deal	Strategic Deal
No discount	1% increase in cost	2% discount
N45 payment terms	N45 payment terms	N30 payment terms
1 year contract	1 year contract	2 year contract
	24/7 customer support	24/7 customer support
		Packer engineers on loan to Universal to help develop next-gen product
		Intro Packer to Universal new product development team for laptops and digital assistants

Negotiation Results

The following week Sanjiv and Mason met with Alex and Packer's COO to negotiate a final deal. When it came time, Sanjiv showed Packer their drafted chart of MEOs and started explaining the thinking behind the alternatives. Both Sanjiv and Mason spoke about each option, detailing the benefits to both companies. As Sanjiv was explaining the details of the third option, "Strategic Deal," the COO of Packer's eyes lit up.

"I like the 'Strategic Deal' option because partnering with a large smartphone manufacturer like Universal on the development of the next-generation phone is very appealing to us. It would boost our reputation immensely. But, the thing is, we just can't do a two percent discount right now. We need to maintain our price in order to meet your manufacturing quality expectations for the cameras. If we give you a discount, we won't make any profit. Margins are already unreasonably thin."

"We have to get some kind of discount, though. If you want to go with the 'Strategic Deal' option, which has many benefits to you, we have to get a price reduction," Sanjiv responded.

Packer's COO could see how volatile the conversation could turn out, so he interjected quickly.

"How about we go with the two-year contract, but we only go with a one percent discount the first year, and then go to a two percent discount the second year? All of the partnership work (e.g., having Packer engineers on loan to develop the next-generation phone, and Universal introducing Packer to their new product development team for laptops and digital assistants) that is included will compensate for this small sacrifice on your part."

Sanjiv and Mason were delighted at this compromise, but said they would have to talk this over and come back with a new MEO. In addition to that, Packer's COO agreed to pay for additional production costs and was willing to take a reduction in profit in exchange for all of the collaborative work that the two companies were going to embark on in the next two years. He was sure that Packer would make their money back in the long run. He was going to bank on the future.

Epilogue

After signing their new contract with Universal, Packer began their 24/7 telephone support line immediately. This helped Universal's public image tremendously as customers began to use and commend this service. Production at Packer picked up with their new resources and Universal was able to launch Skarp 3 on time. Their eager customers welcomed their release and lauded the quality of the new phones and embedded cameras.

Sanjiv attended a Strategic Negotiation workshop to learn more about the methodology. He was able to share his success story with the rest of his class, which personally exemplified how the process was efficient and effective.

Lessons Learned

- When the deal includes Level 3 strategic trades, the value of the overall negotiation dramatically increases. Keep in mind, that the vendor identifies value very differently than the buyer does.

- In industries that are subject to high change and new models such as consumer electronics, involvement in product development is perhaps the most valuable aspect to the relationship between buyer and seller.

Case Study #9 – Wright Agriculture Company

"International Single Source Negotiations–
Germany and China"

Situation Overview and Business Problem

Wright Agriculture Company (WAC) was a fairly new organization. Founded seven years ago, WAC was quickly rising in the U.S. agricultural machinery market, providing economical agricultural, land and garden products manufactured in their own plant in the U.S. At the production plant in Indiana, WAC used large machine tools to cut, drill, and bend metal to create their agricultural equipment products. WAC mostly made specialized equipment, like tractor attachments, but they had recently expanded their line of products to include larger machinery, such as small tractors and combines.

The Industry

Net farm income had steadily increased within the last ten years, mostly due to increased automation and the resulting improvement in productivity. Small- and medium-sized farms had more money to spend. Home gardening was also driving demand for some smaller WAC products. Demand for small farm and garden products was expected to rise by seven to 10 percent over the next couple of years as farmers were spending more to improve productivity and more people were planting home gardens to grow organic foods. The CEO and COO of WAC (brothers Logan Wright and Connor Wright, respectively) had long-term aspirations for WAC to become number one in the agricultural and garden machine market. In order to expand their operations to meet the growing demand, the company had to expand manufacturing. WAC Engineering was charged with making production of farm equipment more efficient with new machine tools and methods. WAC Purchasing was expected to support WAC Engineering by sourcing and qualifying new vendors.

Initially, WAC had been sourcing their machine tools from domestic vendors, but this strategy became more and more expensive (compared to imports of similar tools). So WAC now worked with vendors internationally for the procurement of machine tools and other equipment needed for their production factory in Indiana.

The WAC Purchasing department was an established and professional group, with 14 buyers, two managers, and one vice president. Just about everyone in the department had some international buying experience, even if it was only buying from U.S. distributors of foreign-made goods. The Purchasing department had recently been through Strategic Negotiation training and were using the methods and the Value Blueprint (VBP) tool with some success. They were encouraged to use the VBP by the Purchasing department managers and VP. They were also applying the single source negotiations (SSNs) tools and techniques and found these to be very helpful.

Judy Jiang, one of WAC's Senior Buyers for machine tools, was tasked with supporting Engineering for the acquisition of a new, more efficient machine tool for the Indiana factory. Judy knew that the Manufacturing Engineer, Tex Clark, had already been working with a German machine instruments and controls maker, and he had contacted a Chinese machine housing vendor—both integral parts of the machine tool to make the tool work.

This is going to be an interesting global procurement project, Judy thought, and also a chance to work with single source negotiations strategies. I am going to utilize the Strategic Negotiation methods and blueprinting to manage the whole process.

She smiled; perhaps she would get to go to Germany and China to visit the vendors with Tex. What an adventure that would be! Either way, whether she got to go or not, she vowed to do the best she could on this project and support Tex.

Tex had been working on the engineering designs for the machine tool for three months. He had already sent the preliminary drawings to Zinger Works in Leipzig, Germany, an industrial town known for precision tooling and controls. The machine would require mechanical parts, controls, and software to make it run. Tex was also working with the Chinese vendor, Xufeng, based on a recommendation from a friend who was also a mechanical engineer. Tex's friend said that Xufeng produced high quality cabinets and wiring harnesses for machine tools at very low prices. Tex was evaluating Xufeng to provide the machine housing for the wiring and protective panels. He was hoping that his friend was right about them and that Xufeng would negotiate reasonably. He was looking forward to working with Judy as well, because he had heard that the Purchasing department was using new methods and tools for negotiations. Tex didn't have a lot of firsthand experience with negotiating, and he welcomed this partnership as an opportunity to learn. He also really liked Judy—she was cooperative, supportive and always professional.

Judy came into Tex's office to discuss a plan for the buy. After catching her up to speed on what he had been doing with Zinger and what he was hoping to do with Xufeng, Tex asked Judy about the negotiation process.

"Can you tell me what you learned in the new workshops? Anything useful that we could apply to this particular situation?"

Judy pulled out a handout that she had received on single source negotiations and opened a new Value Blueprint file on her laptop.

"A lot of useful stuff, actually. There was a part of the workshop where we discussed SSNs specifically and we can apply those ideas to Zinger and Xufeng. This Value Blueprint (VBP) tool will also help us capture requirements, priorities and trades throughout the whole process," she said.

"The first step is to figure out what Zinger and Xufeng would each do if we cannot reach an agreement—their 'Consequences of No Agreement,' or CNA. We also need to figure out how to enhance and leverage our value to both of them by identifying why it is important for them that we become and remain their customer. What will Zinger and Xufeng value about their relationship with WAC? What are they losing if they don't work with us? How can we become one of their favorite customers so that they will want to work with us now and in the future?"

"Well, we have never purchased anything from either one of these vendors," Tex said, "So we will have to build a new, strong relationship with both of them."

Judy pointed to the section on the handout about enhancing and leveraging value. "We need to figure out how to transform ourselves into a really great, favored customer by 'looking for terms and conditions that will cost WAC little but that Zinger and Xufeng will value highly.'[14] We should begin by outlining our CNA as well as Zinger's and Xufeng's with the Value Blueprint tool."

"Okay, let's do that," Tex replied. Judy opened the VBP file and showed Tex the list of CNA possibilities from the drop-down menus. "This is really helpful," Tex said. Judy and Tex spent the next 30 minutes discussing CNAs for WAC, Zinger and Xufeng. Because they were dealing with separate vendors and negotiations, Judy opened separate VBP files—one for each vendor. Judy knew these CNAs that they were coming up with were probably not complete, but they were a very good start at blueprinting the two deals.

"This is a great start, Judy. Thank you for showing me this. We are going to have to go to Germany and China to negotiate one-on-one with them, though. We need to visit their headquarters, check them out, and make sure everything is up to snuff. Are you okay with that?"

"Ooh, how exciting! I was hoping that we had to, actually. Traveling was one of the most appealing things about this job for me."

"You know it's just going to be work the entire time, though. We will have little time for sightseeing."

"Oh, well, I'm still excited!"

Judy returned to her cubicle and reviewed the VBP files. It was a pleasure to work with Tex. Not only was he a primary Engineering stakeholder, he had a high bar for excellence in engineering and a good reputation in the company. Judy knew she'd be learning a lot from these negotiations and traveling with Tex.

Per the WAC Travel Policy, before any trip could be booked, international travel had to be approved by her boss, Tex's boss, and the CFO. Judy needed a travel budget for the travel request form, so she called the corporate travel agent to get costs for the trip. Flights to Europe, even in economy class, were particularly expensive. Airfare for two people was going to be nearly $8,000. Then there was the hotel and meals to consider. She worked on the travel budget for nearly an hour and called

---

[14] Brian J. Dietmeyer, "Increasing Your Power in a Single Source Negotiation" (Think! Inc., business negotiation, redefined, 2010).

Tex with the numbers. For the two of them, the trip would cost between $13,000 and $15,000.

It was a pretty hefty cost for one trip, but the new machine tool was going to cost nearly half a million dollars, and they really needed to meet these vendors in person to finalize the design and negotiate the price. Both Judy and Tex got approval from their supervisors for the trip, but they still needed to get approval from the CFO. He balked at the sound of "between $13,000 and $15,000" but after stating their case, he agreed that it was important for them both to go.

Tex had explained, "I know it seems like a lot for one trip, but in the long run, it really isn't. In order for us to make an informed decision on whether or not Zinger and Xufeng are the right companies for us, it is absolutely crucial that we meet the manufacturers in person and evaluate their manufacturing plants. It will be a lot easier to understand how we can make this a better situation for all parties if we see everything and talk to people in person. We need to show them how they'll benefit from working with us, so they'll be more willing to give us what we want and need down the line."

"Okay, okay, you're right. If WAC is going to be number one in the market, then we need to start by sourcing better vendors, you're right. Go ahead and book the trip."

Tex and Judy were pleased, but they soon realized that that was just the easy part. In preparation for the trip and to help inform Judy, Tex reviewed with her what he had been doing with Zinger and Xufeng. Tex had sent both vendors the machine blueprints and specifications; after reviewing those, the vendors would be able to quote their prices to WAC.

"I'll gather available information on line for both manufacturers, too. It will help us as we continue to work on CNAs and possible trades," Judy told Tex.

Both Zinger's and Xufeng's websites had "About Us" pages that listed some of their customers. Using WAC's online account with a business research company, Judy was able to develop a list of references and contacts for each of the customers listed on the vendors' websites. She also asked Tex to request references from both companies. She was planning to interview the senior buyers from each company, to ask them questions about their experience with each vendor. Judy wrote out her list of questions:

- What was your overall experience with Zinger/Xufeng?
- How long have/had you been doing business with them?
- Have you ever had any problems?
- If so, how were those problems corrected?
- What was the quality of the products you purchased from Zinger/Xufeng?
- Did they deliver on time, as promised?
- Would you do business with them again?

After researching the companies and spending the bulk of the next day interviewing references, Judy prepared summaries for both vendors.

Zinger:

- What had been done to date with them
  - Tex had been communicating with them; sent machine blueprints and specifications
  - Tex already had several phone calls with the designers and salespeople at Zinger and he was pretty confident they were able to produce what he wanted
- What she found out in her research
  - In addition to taking custom machine tool orders (like WAC's), they have ready-to-ship accessories, parts, and supplies
  - Zinger has a specialty design team dedicated to working with customers like WAC for specialty machine tools and controls
- What the reference checks determined
  - Excellent quality products
    - Works well with specific and challenging specifications

- Delivered on time
- Customer service is hit and miss—sometimes they address issues quickly and sometimes they take a long time to respond; one reference stated the worst case in which they had to resolve the issue themselves, including redesigning a machine part, after Zinger failed to respond
- They can be a bit rude and rough to deal with

Xufeng:

- What had been done to date with them
  - Tex had been communicating with them; sent them machine blueprints and specifications
  - Tex had had a couple of Skype calls with them, but the language barrier made it difficult to communicate exactly what he wanted
- What she found out in her research
  - Maintaining a strong relationship is important to Chinese companies
  - Xufeng website looked great—it was well-designed but seemed to include a lot of general sales information and very little substance about their capabilities
- What the reference checks determined
  - Good quality products—especially the first items delivered
  - Delivered on time
  - Quality customer service—addressed issues quickly via email
  - References said that WAC "must go to China and deal with them directly"
  - Communications can be difficult—not sure Xufeng understands everything

Next, Judy worked on refining the CNA outline. From this, she could then judge how WAC could become a great customer to Zinger and Xufeng. She started populating the Value Blueprint for each vendor using the information she gathered from her research and what she and Tex discussed earlier.

Consequences of No Agreement (CNAs)

WAC	Zinger	Xufeng
Have to spend more time researching/ contacting alternative vendors	Loss of $300K opportunity for one machine and potential loss for more in the future	Loss of $100K opportunity for one machine and potential loss for more in the future
Delay in machine tool development → delay in WAC product development and releases → loss of potential sales	Loss of a new customer in the small equipment manufacturing market	Additional customer in the U.S., where Xufeng was trying to expand

Judy reviewed the CNAs with Tex and then they discussed how WAC could become a favored customer to both vendors. They agreed that they were going to be amicable and friendly upon meeting the manufacturers—this was the preferred vendor relationship approach at WAC. They also agreed to be firm in what they wanted from both vendors, though, but reasonably so. The way to do this was to identify what valuable things WAC could provide (i.e., how they could fulfill the wants and needs of Zinger and Xufeng); of these items, what they were willing to trade; and figure out what things would cost WAC little but that the vendors would value highly.

Judy and Tex weren't able to pinpoint Zinger's and Xufeng's actual trades just yet (they would have a better idea of that once they met them and talked to them) but they thought it would be best to at least identify WAC's potential trades. They discussed:

- What are Zinger's and Xufeng's criteria for "best customer"?
- How can WAC align with both vendors' best-customer criteria?

According to the single source negotiations handout that Judy showed Tex earlier,

> Best-customer criteria usually includes straight-forward items such as price, volume, delivery, length of contract, and strength of relationship at multiple levels within the supplier's organization. More advanced best-customer criteria may include information sharing, supply management, warehousing, electronic-data exchange, joint-revenue targets, and process-improvement projects.

Using this as a guideline, Judy and Tex drafted a list of WAC's potential trades:

- Reasonable pricing that would allow Zinger and Xufeng to achieve a reasonable profit on the deal
- Prompt payment terms
- Progress payments over three months
- Weekly status calls to review progress and provide guidance and feedback
- Become a reference for Zinger and Xufeng, including allowing the vendors to put the WAC logos on their websites
- Future co-development opportunities for new products

The Trip

Judy had booked the trip for six weeks later. What she hadn't mentioned to anyone was that her parents had emigrated from China to Chicago with their parents in the 1960s and had never been back. She knew she had many relatives in China, but didn't think she would be able to visit any of them on this trip. When she talked to her aging parents about going to China, they were delighted that she would be able experience the culture, even for a few days.

The day to fly to Germany finally arrived. She met Tex at the airport at 6:00 a.m., only to find out that their flight to Frankfurt was going to be delayed for two hours. Judy had been up since 4:00 a.m., had drank three cups of tea before leaving the house, so this just made her even more restless. Tex tried to calm her jittery nerves, although he found it amusing that Judy was getting so nervous over a two-hour delay.

"Hey, hey, it's not that big of a deal. It's just a delay—two hours is nothing. This happens all the time, we'll get there."

"I know, I know…I'm just nervous about this whole thing! I don't want to screw things up."

Tex replied, "We've prepared as much as we can for our side of the situation. We have to focus on becoming the best customer we can be to them. Let's go over our notes while we wait. There's certainly no harm in reviewing."

Over the next hour, Tex and Judy reviewed key points in becoming a great customer to their potential vendors and went over WAC's items for trade. Tex discussed what he expected out of Zinger—he wanted them to focus on the engineering and working with his tight specifications, which was what Zinger was known for. Since this was the first time WAC was using international vendors for a new machine development, he was worried about being able to keep tabs on their progress. He expressed a need for staying in close contact with Zinger by planning to propose a weekly video conference call in which they could discuss how things were going, give Zinger a chance to ask any questions, present any issues, etc.

Next, their review turned to Xufeng. Both Judy and Tex understood that maintaining a strong business relationship was important for Chinese companies. They vowed to make a good impression with Xufeng with friendly, but professional, demeanors and to convey their wants and needs very clearly and literally, as to not get lost in translation. They had read several articles and books about doing business in China and knew they needed to expect the negotiations to go on longer than they had planned. Judy could also speak a little Mandarin and was at least somewhat familiar with the culture according to her parents and grandparents. She wondered how the people at Xufeng would view her as an American-born Chinese.

After exhausting the discussion, Judy felt a bit better about things. Her nerves began to calm and she was able to relax a bit until they were ready to board the plane.

Identifying Anchors

Since Tex had been communicating with the vendors about the machine tool's specifications, both Zinger and Xufeng had already provided some preliminary quotes on the machine parts. Judy knew to ignore these opening anchors however, as they had yet to discuss the details of the deals with the vendors. These opening offers were likely to be in the agreement zone, though.

The suppliers didn't know that she and Tex had been drafting CNAs and discussing potential items to trade. In order to become a favored customer to both vendors, she had to identify and address the needs of Zinger and Xufeng and how WAC could fulfill these needs. If things went well during this trip, she expected to offer prices of about $300K for Zinger's tool and controls and $100K for Xufeng's housing. She and Tex determined that these prices were reasonable targets.

Identifying and Dividing Value

After a long trip, they finally landed in Frankfurt. Tex had been to Germany before and had some experience with driving there. They rented a car and drove several hours to get to Leipzig. Judy scoped out her surroundings as Tex drove.

As they drove into Leipzig and neared Zinger, she thought, *Germany is lovely. Even though Zinger is in an industrial park, the areas around the city are quaint looking and the people have been quite friendly. I hope we have a little chance to look around some more before we leave.*

Judy and Tex spent the entire next day meeting with Zinger and evaluating their manufacturing capability. At end of the day, they then went to work on outlining their potential trades. They had a good idea of what Zinger wanted out of this deal, so they used that as a foundation. To begin, Judy pulled up the brief list of WAC's trades that they had already written up before they left Indiana. She added the potential trades for Zinger to the electronic Value Blueprint.

WAC's and Zinger's Potential Trades

WAC	Zinger
Pricing between $280K and $300K	Discount of 10–15%
Prompt payment	Design assistance from Zinger's best engineers for WAC and for Xufeng
Progress payments	Installation assistance in Indiana at no additional charge to WAC
Provide references including allowing the vendor to put the WAC logos on their website	
Weekly status calls to maintain good communications and for guidance	
Future co-development opportunities for new products	

After dinner, Tex and Judy spent some time developing MEOs for Zinger. Judy was feeling the effects of jet lag so she was thankful that most of their discussion was going to be on how WAC would become a great customer. She was tired.

Identifying Multiple Equal Offers (MEOs)

After doing their prep work in Indiana and outlining each company's potential trades, coming up with MEOs was pretty easy. They settled on two initial MEOs.

MEOs for Zinger

Strategic Partner	Good Relations
$290K	$280K
Progress payments in three increments over three months	N30 after delivery and installation
N30 after invoicing	WAC to provide up to three reference calls for Zinger
Design assistance from Zinger's top engineering team	

Strategic Partner	Good Relations
Zinger to provide installation assistance at no cost to WAC	
WAC to provide up to five reference calls for Zinger	

The next day Judy and Tex presented the MEOs to the CEO and VP of Sales at Zinger. Zinger was very pleased with both alternatives but indicated that they wanted to move forward as a strategic partner. They agreed to the price of $290K, even though they had originally quoted $310K. All of the other benefits of being a strategic partner compensated for the price gap. There were handshakes all around and they had a celebratory lunch at a nearby restaurant. There would be no second round of negotiations. They all agreed on the pricing, terms and Level 3 trades.

"I am going to email my boss," said Judy. "She will be pleased with the outcome."

"And I am going to email my boss and tell him how helpful you have been, Judy," said Tex. "I'll copy the CFO, so he knows what a good investment this has been so far."

Judy and Tex decided to take the afternoon off before their flight to Shanghai the next morning. Visiting a small village just outside of town, Judy bought some souvenirs for her kids and then they had a wonderful dinner at a lovely restaurant.

Shanghai and Pudong, China

The next morning, Judy and Tex left Leipzig for Shanghai.

This is an incredible opportunity to see the world, thought Judy. *I am truly lucky.*

From the Shanghai airport, Tex and Judy took the Maglev High Speed Train into the city and then a taxi to their hotel in Pudong. As with most of the big Asian hotels, this one had a grand marble lobby and spectacular rooms. Judy's room had a wonderful view of the high-rise buildings in Pudong. She texted her husband and kids and emailed her parents. One phrase kept going around and around in her head, *This isn't your grandparents' China anymore.* She felt a bit overwhelmed by the size and energy of the China she was experiencing.

By the next morning, when they met for breakfast, both Tex and Judy were feeling great and ready to go to Xufeng. Judy had been a bit nervous about coming to China—halfway around the world. But what she had seen so far was a spectacular and interesting city and a luxurious hotel. Wow! What an experience this had been so far.

When Judy and Tex arrived at the Xufeng offices, they were greeted by the entire executive team and escorted into a conference room where they were offered tea and bottled water. After introductions of all the people and a welcome presentation by Xufeng, Tex and Judy were taken on a tour of the manufacturing areas. Everything looked okay to Judy, but Tex seemed to be asking a lot of questions and looked a little concerned.

Four of the Xufeng executives took Judy and Tex to lunch at a very nice restaurant and ordered far more food than they could eat. The conversation was light and mostly about families and life in Indiana. The Chinese were curious about America even though most of them had visited California and New York. After lunch they returned to the Xufeng offices for technical discussions. The language differences made it more difficult than it had been in Germany. Here, the people all spoke English, but with a heavy accent that made it hard to understand. Judy found that her knowledge of Mandarin was so limited that it didn't really help her in these discussions.

By 4:00 p.m., Tex and Judy were weary and ready to return to the hotel. In the taxi on the way back, Tex told Judy he was a bit uncomfortable with the way drawings and revisions were handled on the manufacturing shop floor, but overall he thought Xufeng could do the work. They decided to present MEOs the next day.

At dinner, they discussed trades and then MEOs:

WAC's and Xufeng's Potential Trades

WAC	Xufeng
Pricing between $90K and $100K	Discount of 15–20%
Prompt payment	Collaborative work on design between WAC, Zinger and Xufeng
Progress payments	Installation assistance in Indiana at no additional charge to WAC
Provide references including allowing the vendor to put the WAC logos on their website	Additional new product offerings
Weekly status video calls to maintain good communications and for guidance	Introduction to other Chinese vendors
Future co-development opportunities for new products	

MEOs for Xufeng

Strategic Partner	Good Relations
$60K	$50K
Progress payments in three increments starting with a first payment of $20K at the project start	N30 after delivery and installation
N30 after delivery in Indiana	Reference for 3–4 companies
Reference for 2–3 companies	
Design assistance from WAC's and Zinger's top engineers	
Possible co-development opportunities	

Tex and Judy had decided on a max budget of $100K for Xufeng but had read in their research that most Chinese negotiations are expected to start with a low price. Wanting to make sure the offer was in the agreement zone, Judy didn't want to start too low. If WAC was going to trust this vendor over a long period of time, their profit margin would have to be reasonable.

The next morning, Judy presented the MEOs to the Xufeng sales and engineering executives and received only polite nodding of heads; no discussion and no push back. During a break, Tex mentioned that he didn't think the executives could make a decision without consulting the CEO. So, after the break, Tex proceeded with the technical discussions, focusing particularly on engineering drawing control. Judy and Tex left Xufeng early and took a walk along the famous Bund in Shanghai.

"I think we might be dealing with some cultural differences we don't understand," said Tex.

"I think you are right," said Judy. "Let's not make any assumptions until we meet them again tomorrow."

The next day, Judy and Tex again met with a few Xufeng executives in the conference room. It felt like there were going around and around about the same issues and not making any progress. About an hour after the meeting started, the CEO showed up and said he wanted to discuss pricing. He liked the idea of Strategic Partnership and was particularly interested in getting engineering design assistance from WAC and Zinger, but countered on the price. He said the best they could do was $90K. After a few rounds of pricing discussions, they finally agreed on $75K.

Judy was pleased and so was Tex, although he knew he would have to closely monitor the production situation at Xufeng and make more trips to China.

On their final day at Xufeng, Judy and Tex were able to get agreement on the general terms and trades. Judy knew from her dealing with other Chinese companies, that she would need to get agreement in writing, too. There might be some additional rounds of negotiation via email and perhaps another trip to China.

As they lifted off from the Shanghai/Pudong airport late that afternoon, Judy looked out over the city. She knew she wanted to come back and bring her family to experience China.

Negotiation Results

Over the next few months, Tex adhered to his determination of keeping a close eye on Xufeng. Regular conference calls with both Zinger and Xufeng ensured both manufacturers in doing a quality job. Tex was able to help them with any problems they had and it made him more approachable for the vendors to ask any questions outside of the conference calls.

This particular deal was exemplified as an influential case study for use of the Strategic Negotiation methodology at WAC; the Purchasing department heralded Judy as she relayed how she and Tex effectively negotiated with SSNs. The Wright brothers were extremely happy with how things went as it looked like the company was moving in the right direction in becoming a top agricultural and garden machine manufacturer.

Epilogue

Although the negotiation went well between WAC and their two new vendors, there were a few hidden costs that Judy had not considered. For example, importing into the U.S. required assistance from a U.S. Customs broker. This turned out to be a big hassle, especially finance-wise, as the entry costs and duty rates were nearly $3,000 for both entries from Zinger and Xufeng. The cabinet from Xufeng, arriving from China, required special handling and a special truck to deliver it. This was an additional $800.

Judy was disappointed that she didn't consider these hidden costs but she took it as a learning experience. She put it on her checklist for the next negotiation deal, for both existing and new vendors. She and Tex expected to continue with Zinger and Xufeng as both vendors were performing well and she documented that WAC negotiated a good deal. She wanted to establish a long-term relationship with both vendors. Since all three companies were communicating and working so well together, she arranged for Zinger and Xufeng to send representatives to the upcoming international machine show in Chicago in the Fall. They would be showing their quality products to the public and it would also be an opportunity for the three companies to meet in-person again. This would maintain their strong customer-vendor relationship and keep WAC in line as a favored customer.

Lessons Learned

Working with SSNs does not necessarily mean that you are powerless. Researching your suppliers helps significantly as you can better understand their company and industry issues, their CNAs and how you can address their needs and priorities. Understanding this last point is crucial as it can help to make you a favored customer and enhance your negotiating power. Focus on developing valuable trades to make your company a more desirable customer.

Afterword

Through this book, we have attempted to provide you with the fundamentals of the Think! Inc. approach to Strategic Negotiation. But we didn't think it was good enough just to lay out the fundamental ideas and approach so we added the case studies. We hope these stories helped to drive home how the Think! methodology can be used in buying situations across industries. We enjoyed writing them and hope you enjoyed reading them.

Most importantly, we want you to practice building CNAs, developing trades and creating MEOs as part of blueprinting your negotiations. If you have participated in one of our Procurement workshops, you should have an electronic copy of the Value Blueprint. This will provide guidance as you negotiate more value for your company.

We always tell participants in our training that we cannot teach you to be lucky. We can only teach you process and analysis. And with this, we wish you much good analysis!

About the Authors

Rosemary Coates is the Think! Inc. Procurement Practice Leader and President of Blue Silk Consulting, a Global Supply Chain consulting firm. She is the author of 2 books: *42 Rules for Sourcing and Manufacturing in China* (an Amazon.com Top Seller) and *42 Rules for Superior Field Service* (released Fall 2012). She earned a BS in Business Logistics at Arizona State University and an MBA from the University of San Diego. Ms. Coates lives in Silicon Valley and has worked with over 80 clients worldwide. She is on the Board of Directors of the University of San Diego Supply Chain Management Institute. She is also an Expert Witness for legal cases involving global supply chain matters.

Brian Dietmeyer is President and CEO of Think! Inc., a global strategic negotiation consultancy. Think! Inc.'s insight has resulted in several client return on investment analyses of over 200 percent in a less than 12-month period. Mr. Dietmeyer has nearly 25 years of leadership experience in sales, marketing and strategic planning. He is also a sought-after speaker and columnist, author of two books: *B2B Street Fighting* and *Strategic Negotiation*, and founder of Think! Inc. with Dr. Max Bazerman, executive committee member of the Harvard Project on Negotiation. Dr. Bazerman created the concept of MEOs after observing thousands of deals in 25 different countries.

Diane (Minh) Vo helped in the case development and editing of this book. She is a Production Manager at Happy About Publishing. Ms. Vo earned a BA in English from UC Davis and a Master's degree in Library and Information Science from San Jose State University. She lives in the San Francisco Bay Area.